growing up
Inside and Out

Written by KIRA VERMOND

Illustrations by CARL CHIN

For Nicole, who led the way.

Text © 2013 Kira Vermond
Illustrations © 2013 Carl Chin

Owlkids Books acknowledges the financial support of the Canada Council for the Arts, the Ontario Arts Council, the Government of Canada through the Canada Book Fund (CBF) and the Government of Ontario through the Ontario Media Development Corporation's Book Initiative for our publishing activities.

Published in Canada by
Owlkids Books Inc.
10 Lower Spadina Avenue
Toronto, ON M5V 2Z2

Published in the United States by
Owlkids Books Inc.
1700 Fourth Street
Berkeley, CA 94710

Library and Archives Canada Cataloguing in Publication

Vermond, Kira
    Growing up, inside and out / Kira Vermond.

Includes bibliographical references and index.
ISBN 978-1-926973-89-0 (bound).--ISBN 978-1-77147-004-9 (pbk.)

    1. Puberty--Juvenile literature. 2. Adolescence--Juvenile literature. I. Title.

QP84.4.V37 2013   j612.6'61   C2012-908521-9

Library of Congress Control Number: 2013930985

Design: Barb Kelly

Manufactured in Dongguan, China, in March 2013, by Toppan Leefung Packaging & Printing (Dongguan) Co., Ltd.
Job #BAYDC4

A   B   C   D   E   F

 Publisher of Chirp, chickaDEE and OWL
www.owlkidsbooks.com

→ Contents

→ Introduction

Everyone grows up.
But only you grow into you.

Growing up.

It sounds so simple.
Moving in one direction.
Up! Here we go...

But is there really only one way to grow? No way. That's the funny thing about growing up—even though it's something we all do, it's something we all do a little differently from each other. So what does it all mean?

You might have heard that growing up is all about something called puberty. Well, that is a big part of it. Puberty is the time in your life when your body matures and you go from a child to an adult. It lasts a few years, and when it's complete, boys and girls not only look older and taller, but also seem even more different from one another. (You've probably noticed this looking at older kids.)

But that's what's happening to your body. Did you know that there's a whole other world opening up inside your head at this point, too?

Suddenly what people do, what they say, and how you react to them all feel different somehow. It can be surprising. Or a bit confusing. Often exciting. Sometimes stressful. But most of all, these twists and turns are not just about you getting new body hair, bigger muscles, or wider hips. Instead, they are more about your emotions. They happen in your head. In most cases, girls and boys experience roughly the same things as they grow up. The good, the bad, and the just plain weird.

To steady yourself through it all, you need some good advice and, in some cases, a bit of a warning about what's around the bend. And that's what this book is all about.

To give you the best head start I could, I spoke to doctors, psychologists, researchers, professors, therapists, teachers, historians, and even a mathematician (you'll see...).

But most importantly, I spoke to kids. Just like you. Some were too embarrassed to say much; others couldn't stop talking. What all of them had in common, though, was one thing: they didn't really care where the pituitary gland was; they just wanted to know how to survive—and enjoy—growing up. I'll bet you feel the same way.

So growing up is a journey we all make. And like every journey, it has to begin somewhere: with your changing body. It all starts on the next page.

READING THIS BOOK

Growing up is something that takes time. That means that while some of the stuff in this book might be happening to you right now, other things may feel a long way away. Why am I pointing this out?

As a guide to growing up, this is a book that's meant to be by your side for a long time. So if there's something you're reading about that doesn't feel right just now, put it aside. Chances are, you'll be more comfortable reading about it before too long. The point is, there's no reason to rush through growing up—or reading this book!

The incredible, shifting YOU!

Your body is about to change. Hold on tight!

Neanderthals. They thought they were so special. Sure, with their thick skulls, big brains, and stocky caveman and cavewoman bodies, they could adapt to the cold, use tools, and even speak.

Definition, please

Puberty is a normal phase that happens when a kid's body changes into an adult body and gets itself ready for the possibility of reproduction someday.

And here's what else: it's possible they whizzed through puberty.

According to European scientists, Neanderthals were all grown up by the time they reached fifteen. It took a lot of food to get that big that fast, but these primates (not our ancestors, by the way—more like close neighbors) were up to the task, chomping through a high-calorie diet to fuel their lightning-speed rapid growth.

Sound good to you? You're not the only one. After all, puberty can feel like a lot to deal with when everything seems so unfamiliar and new. Who wouldn't want to get through it as fast as possible?

It's true. Puberty can be a confusing time—especially when you don't know what to expect from this new body of yours. How will you look? Will you still feel like you? You and your friends may have already started puberty. Just look around your classroom. Perhaps some kids are suddenly getting taller. Others are maybe getting red spots called pimples. Some girls are developing breasts, and others aren't. Some boys are getting broader shoulders; others are keeping it slim.

A lot of the changes that you see in yourself and your friends at puberty are visible because they're happening on the outside of the body. But although these physical changes look like they're only skin deep, they can actually change how you feel about yourself on the inside. Puberty can make you happy—if you're excited to grow taller, get stronger muscles, or have a deeper voice. Or it can send your emotions into a whirl—if, say, you feel awkward because you're one of the first (or last) in your class to begin going through puberty.

Or maybe you worry that now that it's happening, you'll have to act more like an adult (even though you still feel like being a kid).

But there's good news. For starters, it's not as though any of these changes happen overnight. Puberty is a gradual process that takes years—you'll have plenty of time to get used to it all and to remain "you." What's more, if you've got an idea of where you're headed, there's a good chance you'll feel better prepared for it, and more in control of how you feel about it.

And lastly, it never hurts to marvel at the incredible shifting you! How is all of this happening? Why is all of this happening? Let's find out...

WHAT'S A HORMONE?

Hormones are chemicals that carry messages from organs and glands in your body to your cells. Why are they important here? They're a very big deal when it comes to puberty. Not only do they affect your growth, metabolism, weight, shape, and physical appearance, but they even have an impact on your emotions.

Tip

How to read this chapter

Some body changes obviously apply just to boys and others just to girls. But in other cases, everyone experiences basically the same things. So do you wanna know...

What's up with boys? . . . . Turn the page
What's up with girls?. . . . . .Flip to page 11
What's up with everyone? . . . Start on page 15

Imagine you go to bed one night and wake up the next morning in a place that looks like your house but seems kind of…different. For one thing, the bathroom isn't on the second floor anymore. It's in the basement. And the kitchen sink? It's gone. Okay, this has got to be some kind of alternate reality.

A lot of boys feel like this about their bodies when they go through puberty. Just when you think you know what your chest, face, or even penis look like, they change! Some of these changes are pretty cool. Some are a bit weird. All of them take getting used to. Here are just a few examples:

What's up with your voice?

At some point during puberty, most guys' voices will "crack" or "break." Your voice isn't actually being damaged, though. Instead, it's changing pitch mid-sentence whether you want it to or not.

This change happens when…

1. Puberty hits and the voice box gets bigger and vocal cords grow longer.

2. The whole face grows, too, making larger spaces in your sinuses, in your nose, and at the back of your throat. In a way, the face is now acting like a bass drum instead of a small bongo.

The result?

A deeper voice. (At least some of the time.)

Here's the good news: the whole voice-changing process lasts only a few months, and even then, cracking doesn't happen every time you speak. Once your voice box is done having its own growth spurt, your voice will calm down. That's why you might sound like a little kid one month, and somebody's dad the next.

If it only had a brain

Although there are a ton of jokes about your penis having a mind of its own, those funny stories are not so far from the truth. Your penis is unlike your arms, legs, and wiggly toes. In other words, you usually can't just say to your penis, "Turn left," and it will follow your orders. That's because it's in contact with your autonomic nervous system. That's the network in your body that puts your heart rate and blood pressure on autopilot.

The result?

You're the "I" in "I've got no control over this thing!"…some of the time, anyway. Especially when you're dealing with an erection.

An erection is what happens when your penis fills with blood and hardens. It also gets bigger and stands out from your body. Often it happens when you're having romantic or sexual thoughts, or if your penis is being touched. Although some days it might feel like pretty much anything can set it off.

Heavy lifting.

Getting excited about the weekend.

Waking up.

Even little boys and babies get erections, but once they reach puberty and the body makes more testosterone, the frequency increases. That's normal.

Living a teenage (wet) dream

Erections can happen anytime. Even when you're asleep. In fact, men and boys generally have erections every hour to hour and a half while getting their *zzz*s, although they usually aren't aware of it.

Impulses from the brain during the dream (or REM) stage of sleep cause blood to rush to the penis. And because those impulses are what make the penis hard, it really doesn't matter what you're thinking about at the time.

A. Showing up at school wearing a knight costume.

B. A piece of carrot cake.

C. Your latest crush.

D. All of the above.

Yet sometimes those dreams can take an even more exciting turn, and a boy or man becomes sexually aroused, or turned on. Then wham! Ejaculation. That's when semen—a cloudy, sticky liquid that contains sperm—leaves your body through your penis. It's not much, though. Just a teaspoon or two.

If it happens to you, you'll notice a wet patch on your clothes or sheets. But don't be embarrassed. Wet dreams, also known as "nocturnal emissions," happen to almost everybody with a penis and a load of testosterone. Just go wash up, change, and grab a new set of sheets from the closet if you need to. And if you don't feel like telling your mom or dad the next day? No worries. It's about time you learn to do your own laundry anyway.

Pecs, delts, and more

It's Tuesday morning and time to get dressed for school. Digging around your closet, you pull out your favorite shirt and throw it on. Only one problem; it's way too tight across the chest, and you can almost see your belly button. What are you going to wear now?

Height isn't the only change boys notice when it comes time to buy new clothes. Your old shirts might be feeling a little tighter across the chest and arms. You might even notice that your upper body is taking on more of an

THE BIG SNIP

Every boy is born with a flap of skin (called a foreskin) covering the head (top part) of his penis. Sometimes a boy—usually as a baby—has the foreskin surgically removed. In other words, it is (very!) carefully sliced off by people who have experience with such things: doctors, nurses, and religious leaders. This process is called circumcision. Depending on where you live in the world, circumcision can be either very common or not common at all. So why does it happen?

For some parents, getting their sons circumcised is only natural. It's a religious, cultural, or social thing. (For example, Jews and Muslims make up the majority of circumcised males.) Other families opt for the surgery because they think it's more hygienic (cleaner), or they simply want their sons to look like their brothers, fathers, and grandfathers.

Other parents decide not to get their sons circumcised because they think it's unnecessary and don't want them to be in any pain.

Circumcised penises are less prone to infection, and some organizations believe circumcision can even protect you from getting some diseases. But is being uncircumcised a big deal? No, it's only natural! If you pull back your foreskin (something most boys can do by the time they're five-year-olds) and wash with soap and water, you're good to go.

Either way, forget comparing your penis to anyone else's. It's just important that you're happy with what you've got.

upside-down triangle shape: broader shoulders and narrow hips. You're getting muscles for the first time and looking less and less like a kid.

Unless…you're not. During puberty, some boys start to worry that they'll never grow big and look "cut" like their friends. It's embarrassing, especially if you seem to be the last one in your class to fill out. Maybe you look around the room and notice that the girls all seem to want to talk to the beefy guys, but they treat you more like a brother. You hate that.

How about lifting weights?

Sounds like a good plan, but if you haven't quite reached puberty there's one problem: you'll just be toning those muscles, not building them up. That's because your body needs to make enough of the puberty hormones such as testosterone to build those bigger muscles in your arms, legs, and torso. During puberty, many different growth hormones are made constantly, which is why you get bigger and taller so quickly.

If it hasn't happened to you yet, don't worry—eventually your hormones will kick in. Until then, be active your way. Swim, ride your bike, play soccer, or use rubber resistance bands to do some weight training without as much danger of injury. Eventually, those muscles of yours will grow.

Girls ONLY

Admit it. Your body is cool. Those legs walk you to your best friend's house. Fingers grasp that favorite tuna sandwich. Ears hear the music that makes you feel better after a severely rotten day. You know what else is pretty mind-blowing? Before long, you'll look in the mirror and see a woman staring back at you! You'll see hips, breasts, and hair between your legs and under your arms.

Whoa, whoa. Too soon? These changes might make you feel a bit weird, but it's important to remember that nearly every girl on the entire planet experiences puberty. So then, why all the embarrassment, excitement, and drama over something so incredibly common?

It's a good question. Maybe it's time to take a look at what actually happens to a girl's body when she hits puberty.

Busted!

You've probably heard the strange names that people use to describe breasts. Hooters. Boobs. Knockers. But whatever you want to call them, breasts are a body part with a real purpose: feeding infants. That's why you'll find glands inside you that are all geared up to make milk. We're going to talk in Chapter Two about how girls feel about their breasts no matter what size or shape they are, but for now, let's just stick to the facts about the changes breasts go through.

Breasts get growing

Step 1. Small bumps appear behind the nipple. We call this "budding." Your breast area may start to hurt now. Some girls claim it's a sharp-ish pain; others say it's more of a deep ache.

Step 2. The nipple and the areola (the circle around it) get bigger and darker.

Step 3. The rest of the breast grows bigger and (there's no delicate way to put this) pointier. Time to buy a good bra.

Step 4. Finally, breasts go for a rounder and fuller look. You're done!

Or are you? In reality, breasts never really stop growing, shrinking, and changing. A lot of that depends on hormones, your weight, and even having a baby someday.

"Just be patient"

I know. How many times has a grown-up given you this advice? But they have a point. While a lot of girls are worried about the size of their breasts, their development during puberty takes many years. They grow at a rate that is right for your body. So why get stressed out right now? You probably won't reach your final size until well into your late teen years or even beyond. Besides, small breasts are cool. So are larger ones, and everything in between. Believe it. Confidence makes everybody look good and feel great.

11

The truth about periods. Period.

Okay. So growing breasts is one of the first signs that a girl is going through puberty. You can handle that, right? Hold on. What's that? Is that...blood? In your underpants? Relax, you're not dying. You're not even hurt. You've just got your period—and it's completely normal.

Even if you've been waiting to get your period for what seems like ages, the first time you look down and see a spot of bright red or dark rust can be a bit of a shock. Sure, maybe you're also relieved because your friends are throwing around words like "pads" and "cramps" like old pros, and you've been feeling left out. Or maybe you're worried and anxious because you don't know anyone who has her period yet (at least, no one willing to fess up to it). Whichever way you feel, you've got to admit that getting your period (short for "menstrual period," by the way) is a big deal.

So why does a period happen anyway?

Over the course of a month, hormones give your uterus a push to build up a kind of nest or spongy shell that a baby can use to grow inside. That shell is made out of blood and other nourishing materials. But if there's no baby (known as a fetus before it's born), there's no reason to keep the nest. That's when your body says something like, "All right. False alarm. Everybody out!" And next thing you know...

The fluid-like shell stuff breaks free, squeezes through a small opening in your cervix, and heads for the nearest exit: your vagina.

This doesn't happen all at once, though. It takes a few days. Some days the flow is heavy. Other days it's light. After all the fluid is gone, the cycle begins all over again for next month.

CODE RED. DON'T PANIC!

Got your period? At school? Didn't expect it? Okay, here's what you need to do. Wipe yourself down as best as you can, fold up a wad of toilet paper and stick it into your underwear. It will buy you a little time. Then hightail your way to a trusted teacher or the school nurse. Someone will have a pad or tampon for you. Plus, some schools are now installing small vending machines in school restrooms. So keep a couple of quarters in your desk, just in case.

One more thing. Nearly every woman on the planet gets her period. So if you have to ask for a pad or tampon, it's kind of like saying, "I want to brush my teeth. Do you have any toothpaste I can use?" No reason to be ashamed. At all.

Yup, nope, or maybe?

Even though you now know why a period happens, you probably still have plenty of questions. Here are some likely ones:

Will I have any idea my period is on its way?

Maybe. Sometimes there are signs that your period is about to start in the next few days. Some girls feel funny, like they're hungry all the time, or even a bit sick. Meanwhile, others are completely thrown off guard. They had no idea it was coming.

How long does a period typically last?

Between two to eight days. Some girls and women win the period lottery and get off easy, while others have their period for many days longer.

When I get my period, am I going to bleed buckets?

Nope. It just looks that way. It turns out that the liquid coming out of your body is a lot more than just blood. Health experts call this reddish-brown substance menstrual fluid—that's because it also contains a bunch of other stuff, like:

- cervical mucus
- vaginal secretions
- endometrial tissue

All in all, there's only about one tablespoon of actual blood released over the course of an average period.

Will everybody at school know I have my period?

Nope. Not unless you walk around wearing a sign that says, "I got my PERIOD today!" If you want to keep this piece of news private, just keep your lips sealed. (If, however, you feel like sharing, knock yourself out.)

Do I have to love having my period?

Seriously? Perhaps we've forgotten what we're talking about here. It's okay to think that blood is kind of gross.

YOUR VERY FIRST PERIOD HAS A NAME

And no—it's nothing silly like Aunt Flo or Red Flag. There's actually an official word we use to describe your first menstrual cycle ever: menarche. But I have a confession to make. Up until now, I always thought the word was pronounced men-ARSH. It's not.

The correct pronunciation is: men-AR-kee. As in, "Menarche is a bunch of malarkey."

Hip, hip, hurray!

Here's something else to get used to: your brand-new hips and waist. Up until puberty, girls' and boys' bodies have a pretty similar kid shape. But that all changes when those bodies start making more hormones. Testosterone and a few other growth chemicals heap muscles on boys' bones. And girls? Your main hormone is called estrogen. For the most part, it's created in your ovaries (you'll find them in the lower part of your abdomen beside your uterus, the part of your body where babies grow before they're born). Make enough estrogen and it tips off your body to create a whole new shape.

While testosterone gives boys a more muscular body as they grow up, estrogen uses something else to turn a girl's body into one that's more like a woman's: fat.

Eek! Fat?

Hold it right there. No need to worry. Believe it or not, fat is a *very* good thing at puberty. It's responsible for giving a growing girl a well-defined waist, rounder rear, and larger breasts. Without a little fat on your frame, you would wind up looking like a little kid forever. Probably not the look you'll be going for later on in life!

Besides, wider hips aren't just a result of extra padding. Hormones are also responsible for making the hip bones flare out so they spread. Some girls will notice a big difference in how wide their hips get. Other girls won't notice much of a difference at all.

I'm going to be a model someday, dawling...

There's also the height piece of this puzzle to think about. Let's say you're looking at the growth chart on your bedroom wall and notice something strange. Six months ago, your height was pretty average compared to that of your friends. But now? You're nearly a foot taller.

Before you get your mom to start calling modeling agencies and basketball talent scouts, you should know something. Chances are, that height edge is going to balance out—in particular for many girls who get their periods early.

That's because when kids hit puberty early, the growth plates in their bones close sooner than they do in other kids. So though these kids may grow faster at first, they often end up being a bit shorter than they would have been otherwise. In fact, once a girl gets her period, she should expect to grow only a few more inches.

But just because the statistics tell one story, it still might not be your story. You could wind up being that one person who gets her period at eleven and then keeps on growing until she's six feet plus.

For everybody

Hair we go...

If you pay much attention to the adults around you, you know it's going to happen at some point. Hair. Under your arms. Covering your legs. And the area between your legs? (Known as the pubic area, by the way.) It's going the same route, too. You might even notice hair sprouting above your upper lip. Or if you're a boy, maybe you're still waiting for all that sprouting and growing to start. Either way, most kids grow more body hair during puberty and into their teen years.

And not just in the places you'd expect either.
- Breasts
- Below the belly button
- Back
- Bum
- Toes and upper feet

What exactly is the deal with androgenic—a.k.a. body—hair? It's usually a gene thing, so if this sounds like you, you've got your parents to thank.

Even the hair on the head will change. Or make that the oil glands on the scalp. They become more active and hair can get oily. So remember to give your head a good lather more often than you used to. (In other words, Friday Night Bath Night just won't cut it anymore.)

B.O. and U

Hey, what's that smell? It's body odor, or what a lot of people call B.O. for short.

Up until now, you've probably hardly thought about what's going on under your arms. You just throw on a shirt each morning and off you go. But now that puberty has hit? There's a good chance your underarms feel damp a few hours after you take a shower. You've sweat before, but this is getting ridiculous. And why does it reek?

OK, IS *EVERYTHING* ON MY BODY GOING TO CHANGE?

No. Even though it might feel like your whole body is in the middle of a major presto-change-o, there are bits and pieces of you that stay the same. Your fingerprints, for one (or ten).

Lisa Hicks, a doctor in Toronto, Canada, says your hair color won't change (unless you slap down some cash to dye it) and neither will your eye color. "Your belly button, if you've got an outie, it's yours for good, and vice versa," she says. "And your ears—same old, same old. Unless you pierce them, stretch them, or slit them."

Not that she wants to give you any ideas...

For starters, there is a lot more of it now. Adults sweat more than kids. And the main reason B.O. smells can be chalked up to the fact that sweat is known for making nice with the wrong kind of friends: bacteria.

Luckily, there are a few ways to turn down the dial on stench. You can start by washing your armpits with soap every time you shower or take a bath. Eventually, you'll want to try using a product like deodorant or antiperspirant that stops sweat and odor.

A mirror to our skin sins

So you're looking in the mirror, checking out your beautiful new purple braces, when all of a sudden you spot it. A bump. A red bump. A red bump on your chin that feels absolutely HUGE when you touch it. What is that hideous thing?

Simple. It's a pimple.

Whether you call these common spots pimples, zits, or acne vulgaris (their more scientific name), you've probably got two things on your mind the first time you see one pop up:

1. How did it get there?

2. How will you get rid of it?

Truth is, no one really knows why we get acne, especially in the pre-teen and teen years. Sure, there have been a number of theories floating around about what causes the condition:

WHY DO WOMEN AND MEN
SHAVE?

Great question. And depending on if you're male or female, there's a different answer:

So unfeminine!

Women and girls have been taming the hair on the top of their heads since before Cleopatra's day, but it wasn't until about a hundred years ago that they started to look at their underarm and leg hair and go, "Ew."

So why did underarm and leg hair get the hairy eyeball? One word: advertising.

The year was 1915, and sleeveless dresses were starting to hit the streets and the dance halls. This was great news. A woman could throw on a nice cool dress in the summer instead of draping herself in heavy skirts and long fitted sleeves. It must have felt like slipping into a little slice of heaven.

That is, until magazine editors took one look at all those female hairy armpits and made a big stink. That's when a popular women's magazine ran an advertisement with a young woman, arms raised…showing off her completely hairless armpits.

The ad read:

"Summer Dress and Modern Dancing combine to make necessary the removal of objectionable hair."

Other magazines followed suit and proclaimed that women should shave for hygienic (cleanliness) reasons. Other ads explained that bare pits made you groovy and up with the times. By the 1920s, the point was made.

Meanwhile, leg shaving took a lot longer to catch on because women's dress and skirt hemlines dropped again in the 1930s. Besides, everybody wore tights. Who cared about hairy legs if no one could see them anyway? But the moment short skirts and sheer stockings were back in style a couple of decades later, women reached for their razors again.

At least that's what happened in English-speaking North America and Great Britain. Travel around the world and you'll notice that many women don't get rid of their body hair. Although, as with fast-food chains, more countries are adopting things from western culture…including waxing and shaving.

> There is no biological or hygienic reason to shave, wax, yank, or tweeze. It's all about looks. And it's up to you to decide what you like.

The war on stubble

So now we know why girls and women shave their hair off, but why do guys? After all, for centuries men wore beards even when they had access to straight razors, a kind of sharp knife-like utensil. But that all changed after the beginning of World War I. Not only were men required to shave off their beards if they wanted to enlist in the United States Army, but new "safety razors" were hitting the shelves, thanks to two men:

- William Nickerson, an engineer who helped design the hard, thin, and inexpensive blades

- King C. Gillette, American salesman and inventor

After Gillette hit men with a ton of newspaper and magazine advertisements in the early 1900s, sales took off. Eventually the U.S. government gave Gillette safety razors to the armed forces. Soldiers needed to be clean-shaven so that their gas masks fit properly and protected them from nasty chemicals.

By the end of the war, it's reported that 3.5 million "Service Sets" were being used, and a whole nation decided it was fashionable for men and teen boys to sport smooth skin.

Not everybody shaves

And that might include you. Some religions prohibit men from shaving off facial hair. Others say you can't shave the hair off the sides of your face, either. A number of orthodox religions practice this.

If you belong to a religion or a culture that frowns on shaving, you might feel completely comfortable with your decision not to shave. Or you might feel okay when you're around friends and family who follow the same rules you do, but worry about sticking out from your friends at school. Maybe they even ask you when you're going to get rid of that peach fuzz above your lip.

If all this ribbing is starting to bother you, let your friends know why you don't shave. They'll probably lay off. Or talk to a trusted adult or religious leader. They might have ideas about how to live well in two cultures at once.

bacteria, poor diet, not enough sleep, or stress. Some experts chalk it up to a hormone called androgen, which gives the sebum-producing glands (the same ones that now make your scalp so oily) a workout. The more sebum your body produces, the more acne you get.

Acne causes a lot of related conditions. Think anxiety, embarrassment, and feeling socially awkward. Hey, it's hard to feel like a million bucks when you're covered in what feels like a million little bumps. Studies have even shown that people who are anxious about their skin are more likely to avoid playing sports and getting exercise. That's because they're literally afraid to show their faces in public.

Washing your face more often will help. So will using special acne creams and medications. Pick them up at your local drug store. Or you can even visit a skin doctor called a dermatologist to help you manage the spots.

It ain't when it used to be

NEWS FLASH! A load of studies are telling us that more girls and boys are experiencing first signs of puberty—like breast buds, lower voices, and pubic hair—much earlier than they have in the past. As much as six months to two years earlier, in fact.

Why the shift?

So far, experts are having a hard time pinpointing exactly why kids are developing sooner than previous generations did, but there is no shortage of theories. For example, if your mom or dad was an early bloomer, there seems to be a good chance you will be, too.

Other studies suggest that everything from your diet to your weight could help determine how early you start puberty. Whatever the reason for it—or more likely, the reasons—experts feel that early puberty is a trend that's not going away anytime soon.

The new normal?

In the end, the main issue with early puberty is that it makes you feel different from your friends. And that can lead to a lot of confusion and even embarrassment. In particular, girls who develop adult characteristics earlier report that people treat them differently than before. (This is because their growing breasts aren't hidden in the same way pubic hair can be.) Some boys in the class might start making fun of them. Others could even think it's hilarious to touch their chests or bums. (If anybody does this, tell the teacher—or another adult you trust—right away. No one is ever allowed to touch you without your permission.)

I look too old to feel so young!

Early or not, for a lot of kids going through puberty, losing their kid body can make them feel sad. Maybe you feel this way. You're not ready to grow up… and now it's like you have no choice.

But guess what? You do.

Just because you're growing hair under your armpits doesn't mean you can't act like the rest of your friends do. You're still you. Only hairier!

So go ahead, ask Dad for piggyback rides. Climb trees with your little brother. Throw on your favorite animated movie if that's what floats your boat. You can still be a kid if you want.

And if you are actually looking forward to growing up? That's awesome. Keep feeling that way.

Why is this stuff important?

Knowing what's going on with your body is kind of interesting, but isn't biology the end of the story?

No way. All those changes you're experiencing now—whether it's that acne eruption on your chin, a spontaneous erection, or growing breasts—can influence how you think about yourself. Flip to the next chapter and find why.

THE BIG QUESTION

If you could choose NOT to get your period forever, would you?

THE BIG QUESTION

Do you like the idea of having a lower voice or not?

Body break

You've only got one body. Let's love it!

Quick! Walk up to a mirror and what do you see? A life-sized image of your face and body? Or does the size of your reflection change depending on how far away you are from the mirror? Guess what? Both answers are wrong. For the truth, try this simple exercise:

1. Stand still in front of a mirror.

2. Take a piece of tape or a crayon and mark the top of your head on the glass.

3. Now mark the bottom of your chin the same way.

4. Measure the distance between the two points.

You'll discover that your mirrored reflection is actually pretty small no matter how close you stand—only about half the size of your actual face.

A cool trick, isn't it? But it's not only mirrors that have a crazy way of distorting how we see ourselves. Our brains sometimes get it wrong, too. It turns out that we often see ourselves differently than our friends, family, and even strangers do.

That's no big deal if we don't care how the rest of the world views us. But it can be harder to accept if we place pressure on ourselves to look a certain way.

Let's paint a picture of you

To everybody else, you look like a million bucks. What's not to love?

But to yourself, you look too fat, too thin, too muscular, not muscular enough, too hairy, too tall, too short... too different.

These two images just don't add up, do they? Why do you see yourself so differently than others do? Who is the real you?

Poke. You're right there, silly. But seriously, the pressure to look a certain way is everywhere you look. Where exactly?

Get the media message?

On TV and your computer screen, in magazines, at the movies, on book covers, and on the massive billboards you pass by each day, you're bombarded by images. These are called media messages. Some of them have models. Some have movie stars. Some have good-looking men and women in ads for...mustard?

Using good-looking people to sell everything from tires to movies has been going on for about a hundred years. And since we're only human, we usually respond to such messages. After seeing so many of them, we can begin to think, "That's what a normal person looks like."

Even when not everybody around us looks that way at all.

A world before ads!

To be fair, back in, say, 1867—before ads were *everywhere*—kids were still concerned about what they looked like. But because they were comparing themselves to other real people— not touched-up images—their body standards were far more realistic.

Today, some actors spend hours daily in the gym with personal trainers trying to look a certain way. That's time you could better spend playing soccer. Or reading comics. Or hanging with friends. (Or, yes, doing your homework.) Either way, spending your whole day in a gym isn't realistic. Or fun.

Being real and having a good body image (how you see your body) is a big part of loving growing up. Yes, there are a lot of messages out there that can distort that image. But as it turns out, these messages aren't so powerful once you realize how they work. Let's see how!

A LITTLE BOOST

What's not to loathe about a clothing store's changeroom? The tight space, trying on endless pairs of jeans. It's a pain, all right—until you spot a decal stuck to the fitting-room mirror. It says something uplifting like "You: Absolutely No Photoshopping Necessary" or "Yes, You Do Look Phat in That." These little stickers were the brainchild of About-Face, a San Francisco– based organization that runs workshops teaching teens how media messages mess with kids' self-images.

Get 'em while they're young...

Forget the parts of the body we can all see. Advertising even has a hand in shaping how people feel about what's happening inside their bodies. In the case of girls, that's maybe best shown in periods (a.k.a. menstruation).

Way back in the 1920s, menstrual pad manufacturers hit upon one of the best ways to turn women into customers for life: go after girls who were just starting to menstruate. Once they got used to one brand, young girls would be more likely to stick with it as they grew up. But how would companies reach this new audience?

Read all about it

Make a bunch of pamphlets to teach girls the ins and outs of all things related to menstruation. Oh, and at the end, slip in the hard sell and tell the reader to go out and buy your brand.

In one 1929 Kotex pamphlet, called "Marjorie May's Twelfth Birthday," her mom hands Marjorie something she wants her to check out.

"Now, darling, take one of these pads, for I want you to examine it while I finish telling you how nature is soon to provide you with the wonderful purification, which it performs to keep your new physical development free from waste."

Weird right down to the kooky grammar, right? Yet even with the bad writing, it's easy to figure out that the last thing the company wanted was to scare girls off. Instead, they wanted them to think about their periods in two (conflicting) ways:

1. Something that is pretty fabulous.
2. A problem that needs a solution.

When you think about it, that's pretty much how advertisers still address periods today (and shaving, deodorant, makeup, bras, and on and on).

THE TALK
WITH LYNN PERIL, POP CULTURE HISTORIAN AND AUTHOR

Q: When big companies started selling products like pads or tampons years ago, did they actually change the way girls and women think of themselves?

LYNN: Yes, that's absolutely true. The message was, "You have to be happy about your period or there is something wrong with you. Oh, and by the way, your body is going to be doing this thing that is going to require extra care or you're not going to be fresh and sweet and dainty."

Q: So have we come very far since then?

LYNN: Things have changed, but now it's all about "We're here to make your period fun! We're going to make fun commercials, and we're going to make fun products too!" So companies are still trying to dictate the mood around menstruation, but they're more savvy. They know they can't be so incredibly heavy-handed.

Boys feel it, too

Of course, this stuff affects a lot more than just young girls looking to buy their first tampons. Boys and men get hammered with similar media messages. In fact, studies tell us that some boys feel almost the exact same anxieties girls feel, but with a few differences.

WORRY-O-METER!
(Can you spot the difference?)

GIRLS WORRY ABOUT
    height
    being overweight
    skin complexion
    hair and dress style

BOYS WORRY ABOUT
    height
    being underweight
    skin complexion
    hair and dress style

Do you see it? Right. While girls are expected to look thin, boys—at least according to images we encounter now—are supposed to have broad, chiseled bodies. The result for some boys? They try to "solve" their body by controlling what they eat, taking supplements, and downing power shakes. What they don't do? Talk about their body worries with friends. Of course, that's something girls do all the time...just not always in the best way.

Stop the fat talk, girls!

How many times have you overheard (or been a part of) this conversation?

Friend 1: I'm so fat.

Friend 2: You are not. I am.

Friend 1: What are you talking about? You're so skinny. But look at my legs. They're huge.

Friend 2: No, you're the one who's teeny-tiny. My arms are massive...

And around and around it goes.

Finally, someone is looking into why so many girls and women engage in "fat talk." A research paper published in the *Psychology of Women Quarterly* revealed that a whopping 93 percent of teens and college-age women complain about their size with their friends, even when they're already a healthy body size.

A little reassurance

It came out that a lot of the time, girls and women are talking this way so they can get reassurance that they're not actually fat. They say, "I'm so fat," just to hear the words "No, you're not." Only one problem: fat talk can actually make us feel worse, not better. Trash talking your body just reminds you that you're not perfect, and suggests that it's okay to feel bad about how you look.

You know what? It's not. Feeling great about your super-cool body is a much better solution. So take care of it.

Make it strong and healthy. And here's one more possibility to think about: you might hate your toothy grin, the bump on your nose, your full hips, or the birthmark on your calf, but you know what? All those so-called imperfections are actually the unique things about your body that make you…you! And if you asked friends, they'd likely be some of the most memorable (and favorite) parts of you.

So if your best friend wants to talk fat or diss your collective parts, tell her you both look great and change the topic. Nobody should talk trash about your body. Especially not you.

THE TALK WITH MOSS NORMAN, PROFESSOR OF KINESIOLOGY AND RECREATION MANAGEMENT, UNIVERSITY OF MANITOBA

Not long ago, if you'd asked experts how boys felt about their bodies, you'd probably get a pretty typical answer: "They don't."

Huh? That was Moss Norman's reaction, too. The Canadian professor couldn't believe that boys were all okay with how their bodies looked. It certainly wasn't how he'd felt when he was a kid.

"I was a competitive swimmer and had these big, big thighs. So my jeans never fit. I worried it meant I was fat," he says now. "All my friends were skinny and little, and here I was with these quads. When I was twelve or thirteen, I hated it!"

So a few years ago, he decided to find out how boys feel about their bodies today. He sat down with thirty-two guys from Toronto aged thirteen to fifteen and started asking them questions about celebrity bodies. That broke the ice, and soon the boys came clean about their own body issues. Here's what he discovered from numerous interviews:

- Most boys worry about some part of their body but don't want anyone to know. They keep it bottled up inside.

- They don't think big, beefy, muscle-bound bodies are the way to go. It's not like a fifteen-year-old can have that body anyway, they said. It's unnatural.

- They simply want an average body that doesn't stand out. They want to be normal (although everybody seems to have a different idea about what normal means!).

Moss says that our whole society is going to have to change before boys feel comfortable coming clean about how they feel about themselves.

"In our culture, men's bodies are implements to be used, whether for sports or at work. They're not to be worried about, nurtured, or protected," says Moss.

In other words, it's okay to think about your body as more than a pair of legs to kick a soccer ball or hands to play the violin. And if you find yourself worrying about a part of your body because you think it doesn't measure up? That's okay, too. Being anxious about your big swimming thighs, for example, doesn't make you less masculine. It makes you human.

The trick is to be honest about your feelings without letting your body worries take over your life.

Bad body image goes deep

Of course, we can't blame poor body image on advertising and media alone. It's not that simple. There are a lot of other reasons why people can feel crummy about their bodies. They might already suffer from depression (this is severe sadness and hopelessness that lasts for a long time—you can read more about depression on page 48). Or they're anxious in general and worry about everything—including any flaws they have, both real and imagined.

Whatever the causes, some girls and boys respond to these pressures by developing eating disorders. These are serious medical problems that make them starve themselves, vomit their food, or exercise to exhaustion.

Anorexia: Someone with anorexia has an intense fear of gaining weight. He or she thinks about food a lot and eats less and less. This person might be dangerously thin but worry about looking fat anyway.

Bulimia: This is no fun at all. A person with bulimia eats huge amounts of food, feels terrible and depressed, then vomits it all back up again. The cycle can go on and on, hurting the throat, and destroying teeth, and it can even lead to ruined vocal cords, painful stomach ulcers, irregular heartbeat, dry skin, and loss of hair! Sometimes bulimics misuse laxatives and other medicines to get rid of the food they eat. (Yup, by pooping a lot.)

Compulsive overeating: Not all eating disorders are about getting food out. Sometimes people feel like they have to eat all the time and can't stop even when they want to.

Taking supplements: Some boys who feel their bodies are too small or not muscular enough try to tackle their body problems on their own and drink protein shakes or take supplements. They hope that these products will help build up bulk. Problem is, a lot of them haven't been tested fully, and no one knows what they will do to a kid's body over the long term.

Compulsive exerciser: She used to love running cross-country races against kids at other schools. He couldn't wait to hit the soccer field with friends as his parents clapped and cheered him on. But now? She can't seem to sit still and heads out for runs more than once a day. He wants to get bigger, so he lifts weights for a few hours after school, passing up time with friends so he won't miss a session. Compulsive exercisers feel they have to keep moving. They feel anxious and guilty if they don't exercise on schedule.

Who does it?

While only a small number of people ever develop a full-blown eating disorder, about half of all girls and women at some point do unhealthy things to control their weight. More boys are feeling pressured to control their eating and exercise, too. All of these disorders, as well as regular old unhealthy thinking, have one thing in common, though: low self-esteem.

The good news is that there are tons of people who specialize in helping kids with anorexia, bulimia, and extreme exercise habits. You'll find some resources to help you at the back of this book.

Below the belt for boys

Okay, so some boys worry about their height, weight, and acne. But there's another part of the body that often gets scrutinized, too: the penis. Maybe you were changing at school after gym last week and noticed that other boys' penises looked different from yours. Or maybe your buddy is going around bragging that his penis is huge compared to everybody else's. You don't know what to believe, but either way, you worry that the size or shape of your own penis isn't normal.

Is any of this logical? Time to break it down.

The truth #1 The penis is really just another part of the body. When was the last time you worried about the size of your middle toe or the length of your femur bone?

The truth #2 The penis gets a lot more attention than, say, eyelashes or elbows because it is usually hidden away. It's kind of mysterious, so it's easy to fixate on what everyone else's might look like.

The truth #3 From hilariously raunchy movies to boasting friends, you're getting hit with messages from some unreliable sources. According to them, it's all about being bigger and longer if you want to be considered more masculine, or manly. It might make for some funny films, but are these messages even correct? No.

The truth #4 A penis is an easy thing to brag about because anyone can say anything about what they've got—and who's going to know the difference? In the meantime, their boasting has you worried that you're not good enough.

The truth #5 Even if you do happen to see someone else's, there's not much of a relationship between the size of a flaccid (limp) penis and how big it will get when it's erect (which most boys are more anxious about anyway). Some will grow only about a quarter inch (half a centimeter). Others will double in size. That guy beside you who looks big now may stay about the same size when erect. Meanwhile, your friend with a penis on the average side could gain a lot of length and girth. According to some studies, most penises are happy to stay somewhere in the middle.

The truth #6 You boys are not the only ones who worry about this stuff. Girls may not brag about what they've got going on in their underwear, but many get seriously anxious about the size and shape of their breasts. Too full, too flat, too big, too tiny—you name it. In particular, a lot of girls worry that their breasts are too small simply because movies, Web sites, and even friends tell them that big is where it's at. (Sound familiar, boys?) But the truth is, whether you're talking about penises or breasts, biggest is not actually best.

Here's the ultimate truth

The penis you have is 100 percent, completely and absolutely great. Penises come in a range of shapes and sizes, and every one is different. Besides, girls don't care at all about what you look like. (In fact, ask a bunch of girls, and they'll tell you they just don't get why guys are all hung up on penis size. They think it's really, really strange.) And in the future, when you're finally ready to be intimate and share that part of your body with someone, that person won't care about your size: big, small, or somewhere in between. Your future partner will be attracted to you—the whole package, including your kindness, sense of humor, and superhuman ability to whip up a tasty dinner from scratch—not just one single part of your body.

Above the belt for girls

Got it. A lot of boys worry that their penis doesn't measure up. While that might seem a bit strange to girls, as mentioned before, they have some worries of their own. And they come down to two little words: breast size.

This is your life #1

Ugh. Gym class again. Up until last year you loved to get in on the throwing, sprinting, and jumping action. But now? You'd rather park yourself on the sidelines than run out onto the field.

That's because ever since you had to ditch a training bra for a bigger one, a bunch of boys began saying things that make your face red and give you an uncomfortable, creepy feeling inside. All you want is to just go back to playing soccer and having a good time…instead of feeling like everybody's watching your chest as you score a goal. So embarrassing!

This is your life #2

Turn to the left. Turn to the right. Sigh. No matter how much you want it to happen, your breasts just aren't growing much at all. And now that your friends are all heading to the mall to try on bras this weekend, it's just that much worse. You had to come up with a fake excuse for not going. Your mom keeps telling you that she was flat, too, but that doesn't make you feel better at all—because she still is. So embarrassing!

Is either case better?

See? Feeling too big or too small can really rattle a girl. So it's important to remember that puberty causes breasts to change. In other words, you might be flat today, but within six months, you'll be hitting the mall to buy a new bra… again. Or if you worry about standing out because your breasts are bigger than everyone else's, just know that other girls will be catching up soon. Give it some time.

UNDER THE KNIFE!

Hate the way your ears stick out? Wish your chest were smaller? Can't stand your nose? We all have something we don't like about our bodies. But would you agree to have a doctor give you an operation to do something about it? According to the American Society for Aesthetic Plastic Surgery, kids under the age of eighteen made up about one percent of all plastic surgery operations in 2010—equaling 125,397 procedures. While some of the children had medical conditions they needed to have repaired, a small number did it for cosmetic (beauty) reasons.

THUMBS UP

- Having surgery to, say, make your ears stand flat against your head might give bullies one less reason to bug you.

THUMBS DOWN

- These same kids will figure out pretty fast that you've had an operation, so now they have something new to pick on.

THUMBS UP

- Breasts that are too big can hurt your back and make it difficult to run and play sports at school. Surgery can help you feel more comfortable.

THUMBS DOWN

- Because you're still going through puberty, no one knows how your body will eventually end up. Maybe your larger breasts will seem in proportion with the rest of your body when you're grown.

THUMBS UP

- Having a smaller nose might make you feel more normal.

THUMBS DOWN

- Surgery is expensive—and some studies show that surgery doesn't make everybody feel better over the long haul.

Because some kids you see on TV and in magazines and movies have had plastic surgery to look the way they do, you might think that operations are normal for kids and teens.

BUT HERE'S THE REALITY

According to the American Society for Aesthetic Plastic Surgery, only a very small number of kids go under the knife to get a new nose, ears, or other body part. And most importantly, surgery isn't about accepting—or loving—who you are. In fact, it's the opposite!

Your inside helps your outside

Worrying about how you look is really common. Nearly everybody feels anxious from time to time about how they look to other people. But that doesn't have to be the only way to feel. Instead, try these tricks to build a positive inside view of your awesome outside:

- **It's not real.** If you're bummed out that some model or actor looks better than you, take a moment to reflect on the image you see. Is it even real? Has the photo been altered to make her skinnier or him more muscular? Is anyone's face ever that perfect without help from a makeup artist or a computer?

- **But this is.** Next time you hit the mall or amusement park, take a look around you. What do you see? Real people, right? Now count how many of them look like models and actors. Most people don't.

- **Health over looks.** Your body is an incredible thing. Each cell does something cool to keep you breathing, eating, sleeping, running, and acing tomorrow's test. Concentrate on what your body can do, rather than what it looks like.

- **Be active.** There's something neat about exercising and playing sports. It makes you happy. And healthy. And gets you to like your body more. Lots of studies show this is true. Why not test the theory yourself? See you on the field!

You can talk to your parents

Don't get me wrong. I can understand why you might not want to. They're embarrassing, nosy, and full of rules. But guess what? Your parents love you more than anyone else on the entire planet. So they may be the perfect people for further advice about the body issues that we've discussed. The same goes for talking about your feelings and even sex. And though it can be awkward starting the conversation, you can also trust them to keep a secret. Bank on it. Still, these are big issues that can push a lot of hot buttons—in adults and kids! So it helps to hatch a plan before springing a question or asking for an opinion.

Tip 1: Pick the right time.
Don't choose the moment when everyone's rushing out the door for school and work to ask your mom about birth control or wet dreams. Instead, wait until things are calm and you have privacy. A long car ride is a good choice.

Tip 2: Lead into it.
There's an art to asking tough questions. Here are a couple of ways to lead into what you really want to ask:

"We're going to be talking about sex in school tomorrow, but I don't know much about it."

Or

"Do you remember what it was like when your body started changing?"

Tip 3: Choose one.
Some adults are very uncomfortable talking about puberty and sex, so choose the one who seems more open and makes you feel more comfortable. If neither parent seems willing to answer your questions or listen to you, find another person you trust. A best friend's mom or dad. An older sibling or cousin. A favorite teacher. A school coach. A guidance counselor.

Remember, you might not always agree with everything these people say—and they may not have all the answers—but know that they're doing their best to keep you healthy, happy, and safe.

THE BIG QUESTION

What would happen if you looked in the mirror and liked what you saw? How would it change your life?

WANTED: Self-esteem

Where did the good times go?

Just when you thought it was safe to look in the mirror without feeling crummy about yourself, guess what comes along? **Self-esteem zappers!** You'll know it when you come across them, too. They're the people, situations, and even ideas we encounter that make us second-guess who we are deep down. Maybe you've already come across them before…

Girls aren't good at math.

Boys don't cry.

Girls don't play sports.

Boys don't hug.

Definition, please

Self-esteem is related to how we feel about ourselves. It's not about how we actually look but how we feel about our looks. It's not about how smart we really are but how we feel about our intelligence.

Self-esteem zappers do a real number on kids growing up because that's the time when bodies, brains, and attitudes change. This means looking at the world around you and using that information to try to figure out who you are. If that information is positive and gels with how you already feel about yourself, cool. You'll feel secure, healthy, and happy.

31

But if it is negative (like the zappers on the previous page), or doesn't seem to reflect your personality or how you feel about the world, it can make things topsy-turvy and really uncomfortable.

The information we receive can also make us feel as though we have to act like someone else just to fit in. These zappers may hit girls and boys slightly differently, but the result is the same: kids feel out of sync with who they *really* are. And even if we can't say exactly why, we know that feels wrong.

Girls and self-esteem

Let's delve a little deeper and look at how self-esteem zappers can affect girls.

Who actually looks like that?

It's nearly impossible for anyone to look like the girls and women portrayed in the media. But because those images are everywhere we turn, it's hard not to get swept up in them…and to feel bad when our own images don't reflect the world of computer touch-ups. Like body image, self-esteem can take a hit when we get caught up in media messages.

Other kids can be mean

Can you imagine your mom going to work and having to hear her coworkers whisper "She's so ugly" when she walks by them? No way! But it happens at school all the time. That kind of bullying is a lot for anyone to take without feeling anxious, worried, and bad about herself.

Not every girl feels this way, but some start to buy into the idea that it's not cool to be known as the most intelligent person in class. One study from Miami University even showed that while smart boys were thought of as some of the most popular, creative, and funny kids in class, smart girls were considered the least popular and were called moody, aloof, and bossy. Ouch. It's time to show how dumb this stereotype is. Smart IS smart, girls.

It doesn't add up

Maybe you've never thought of it this way, but math can lead to some pretty sweet jobs down the road. Math helps build airplanes, makes computers work, and solves big climate change conundrums. You need math to become a doctor and an astronaut. Many CEOs of large companies have math and science degrees instead of business degrees.

Want to keep your options open? Forget the stereotype that girls aren't good at math. It's even not true, you know. A 2009 study that looked at the issue on a global scale showed the world that girls are just as competent at math as boys if they're given the same opportunities and encouragement.

But that's the trick, isn't it? Everybody's got to ditch the view that girls and math don't mix.

Why math matters!

Fiona Dunbar is a math professor at the University of Waterloo in Canada. She's also involved in the university's Think About Math seminar for Grade 9 girls. She's convinced that most girls would be a lot more positive about math if they knew a few things about the subject.

1. **Yes, math is hard!** It's supposed to be. No one gets the answer right away. In fact, math is a lot like playing the piano. Few people can sit in front of a new piece of music and play it perfectly. It takes time and patience.

2. **But don't ask for help right away.** Fiona says girls feel more comfortable asking for assistance than boys. That's great if you need directions—not so great if you want to figure out a math problem. "The sense of accomplishment you get when you figure it out on your own is important," she says.

3. **Be gentle on yourself.** In other words, don't panic if a math problem is tough. Often math is a lot like setting up a row of dominoes: make a mistake and they all fall down. Just go back and figure out where you started to lose your way. No big deal.

4. **Perfectionists need not apply.** "I see it in my class. The boys will put up their hands and say something ridiculous, but have no problem saying

it. Whereas my girls will wait until they're 100 percent positive they have the right answer first," says Fiona. But math is supposed to be about taking risks and making mistakes at first. That's how problems are solved.

WHY PLAY SPORTS?

A lot of girls give up sports in high school, even if they enjoyed them as kids. But there are so many reasons to keep at it! One University of Florida study revealed that active girls have better body images, as well as more self-esteem and trust in other people. They learn a lot of life skills—and are pretty fit, too!

Believe your own hype

By looking at the messages and images around you with a critical eye, you start to realize they're not real. So why bother trying to measure up to something that isn't true in the first place? And if you're starting to feel like you're losing touch with what makes you special, remember that a lot of girls feel good about themselves through their teen years and beyond. They have unique strengths that help them through. For instance, girls generally feel better about how they do academically than boys do. Girls tend to have great social skills and are less likely to drop out of school. Ups and downs always happen, but these are amazing things to focus on.

And now on to the boys...

Ugh. It's 7:23 a.m. Time to get out of bed. But all you want to do is turn over and go back to sleep. Not that your mom is going to make it easy. She keeps yelling up the stairs at you to get a move on. You're going to miss your bus. You won't have time for breakfast. Blah, blah, blah. The usual stuff.

That's when you remember your math test. The one you forgot to study for.

Double ugh. Now a black, wormy feeling settles in your chest. And what's worse? You know that when your mom sees your poor test mark, she's going to start asking you all kinds of questions about how you're "feeling."

That's right. Feeling.

Putting it into words

Ever feel like you don't know how you feel? Or maybe you know exactly what that emotion is—excitement, worry, anger—but you think other kids would make fun of you if you expressed it or talked about it? It's not just you. A lot of boys feel the same way. Because let's face it, there are a lot of messages floating around you that are pretty confusing:

- Boys don't cry, even if they're sad. (But anger is okay. That's manly.)

- Boys aren't supposed to be afraid or ask for help.

- You should be smart, but not too smart.

- Only girls have mood swings.

- All boys like sports.

- Fighting is the way to solve problems.

There are a whole bunch more of these "rules" out there, but you get the idea. Sadly, a lot of people—teachers, parents, and even other kids—believe these messages even though they don't reflect how real boys feel and act. Instead, the rules are a part of an old, tired-out way of looking at how boys and men are supposed to behave.

It's all bogus. Everybody gets sad from time to time because life isn't always easy or fair. A pet dog dies. A best friend moves away. Parents get divorced.

It would be strange if we didn't get bummed out over this stuff.

All about timing

When you were a little kid, you probably felt pretty comfortable expressing your emotions. You snuggled up to your mom and asked for a hug, or you cried when your helium-filled birthday balloon floated away.

But then something happened.

34

- Some of your friends started making fun of a kid who cried when he slipped on the ice at school. You realized that unless you wanted to get razzed, you better keep your tears inside.

- Or maybe your favorite uncle told you to "man up" one night while camping when you told him you were still afraid of the dark.

- And don't forget your favorite action movies. None of the heroes ever act worried or emotional. It's stiff upper lip all the way—even when it looks like they're about to die in an alien attack!

Let me choose my words

Other messages are much more subtle. For instance, one study out of Emory University in Atlanta, Georgia, looked at how parents talked about emotions with their three-year-old kids. When moms and dads spoke to their daughters, they used a lot more "feeling" words than they did with their sons. They also talked more about sad things that had happened to their daughters. Some experts wonder if boys, even little ones, just aren't getting the vocabulary they need to talk about what's going on inside.

When all of these issues come together, a lot of boys who are reaching puberty discover that these ideas make life tougher. They're scared that other boys will call them a "wuss," or worse, just because they want to hug their friends or walk to school with their mom or dad. Who wants a label like that? Sometimes to fit in, it feels a lot easier to not care about feelings and act tough instead.

That's tough

Fact is, acting tough—when you don't feel tough at all—is only a quick fix. And after a while, pretending you're something you're not can be exhausting... and saps a lot of good feelings you do have about who you really are.

The real truth: there's nothing wrong with wanting to make connections with other people. Think about the last time you watched a game on television. Notice how often players on sports teams hug? They're in the moment and are proud of one another. It just seems natural to reach out and, well, smack someone on the back, right? It feels good, and it's part of being human. Plus, it takes a lot of courage (and strength!) to be different from what's expected of you.

So hug away there, tough guy!

WHEN IN ROME...

Or Israel, or a lot of different countries around the world, it's no biggie for men and boys to be touchy-feely with each other. No one looks at you funny if you give your friend a good, long, heartfelt hug. As Samir Khalaf, a professor in Lebanon, once told a reporter at the *New York Times*, "[Holding hands] is a sign of solidarity and kinship."

Rules and expectations

The point is, feeling good about yourself is all about looking—really looking—at the messages and stereotypes we all come across on TV, at school, and even around the dinner table at home. Do they make sense? How do they make you feel?

Are you ashamed because you cried when you hurt your arm in gym today? *Zzzt! Bogus boy attitude.*

Do you think you've got to be pretty to be liked? *Zzzt! Think again, girl.*

While you're working on that, there are lots of tips and tricks you can use to get your self-esteem back and act like the real you, too. Here are just a few:

Try something new. Have you always wanted to learn to play a musical instrument? Ask your parents to sign you up for lessons, or simply check out YouTube. There are tons of awesome lessons online. Breaking out of your comfort zone is all about learning to live with less fear and embarrassment. (Plus, playing an instrument makes you cool.)

Set a goal. Then follow through. There's nothing like saying you're going to run a 3-mile (5-kilometer) race, training for months, and then crossing the finish line. Yes!

Stop beating yourself up! So what if you got a C- on your last test. It's possibly just a sign that you need to either study harder next time or ask for help. By the way, a lot of A-students aren't tomorrow's Einsteins. Some famous studies have shown that people who are really persistent (keep working at something even when they hit a big snag) are more likely to be successful than kids who give up sooner. In other words, while school obviously comes easy to some students, others study until they understand the material, even if it takes a long time. Something to think about.

Choose who you want to be. I'm not going to tell you to "just be yourself." We've all heard that phrase a hundred times and is it ever all that helpful? If we all felt comfortable in our own skin, no one would be struggling with self-esteem! Instead, if you're going to compare yourself to other people and want to be like them, choose wisely. Find someone who already makes you feel confident and happy, not someone who makes you feel bad for failing to measure up.

THE BIG QUESTION

What are the three words that best describe you? Are they positive or negative? Why?

What's up, brain?

Why emotional roller coasters are no day at the park.

Just five minutes ago, you were crazy happy. You got an A- on that science test you forgot to study for, you've patched stuff up with your best friend again, and even your coach is being cool.

But now? You are mad. No. Scratch that. You're furious! Why does your mother have to ruin…your…life… every…single…day?

Okay, cut.

Ever feel this way? One moment everything is awesome, and then in two seconds flat, you're sad, mad, or just plain fed up. You've probably figured out that puberty can sometimes feel like one great big emotional roller coaster. That's because your thoughts and emotions are changing just as much as your body.

Why is this happening? In the past, experts blamed so-called raging hormones for running through kids' systems and messing up their ability to think clearly.

But don't just blame the hormones! Changes in your brain seem to have a lot to do with how you feel and act, too. Ready to read about some scientific studies that shed light on the emotion-brain-hormone connection? Of course, you are! So let's keep reading.

HOW ARE YOU FEELING NOW?

- **Big emotions.** You don't just kind of like something. Either it's the best thing ever...or it's 100 percent lame (sometimes both pretty quickly).

- **The same goes** for your family, your teachers, and even your friends. Five minutes ago, you were playing Uno with your little sister and laughing like crazy. Now you're screaming at each other and Grandma is playing referee.

- **Body weirdness.** Your body is changing fast, so you feel self-conscious about it and tense. Or it's not changing fast enough.

- **Enter the crush.** What's up with that feeling in your stomach whenever a specific girl or boy in your class looks at you? You've never felt that before, but it's exciting. (More in Chapter Seven!)

- **Being bummed out.** You didn't make the basketball team. Last year you wouldn't have cared that much. But now? You're feeling embarrassed, angry, and depressed. What's going on?

- **Feeling crazy.** All of a sudden you can't sit still. You want to live life BIG. That means taking your sled to the top of the biggest hill in the city and zinging down...backward. Or sneaking out of the house with your friends at midnight to egg your nasty neighbor's house. There's a certain thrill in the possibility of being caught.

Hormones? Brain? Why not both?!

For years, most scientists thought the brain was fully matured (developed) by the time a kid turned twelve. That squishy organ in your head was not only as big as it was going to get, but it also had all it needed to think like an adult. Since then (with the help of MRI machines that can take detailed pictures of the brain), scientists have been singing a new tune: your brain at twelve isn't like a grown-up's at all. It's possible that it is changing until you reach twenty-five.

In fact, it seems that some of the most critical brain changes happen when girls are about eleven years old and boys are about twelve and a half. That's possibly why some things are harder to learn around this age.

By the time you turned six, your brain was between 90 percent and 95 percent of its adult size. But you were born with as many neurons (nerve cells) as you're likely to ever have.

Something shocking

A few years ago, a team of New York researchers came up with a complicated mouse test. The rodents had to find ways to avoid a moving platform that gave a mild shock. (Don't worry. The mice weren't hurt, just a little stressed.)

It took some practice for the mice to learn to avoid the platform. Prepubescent mice (little pipsqueaks that hadn't reached puberty yet) mastered the task quickly. So did older mice. But the mice going through puberty? Forget it. They were stumped.

Some scientists think this temporary dip in intelligence happens at puberty because of chemical changes in a part of the brain called the hippocampus. When mice hit the age of five weeks—mouse puberty—learning is more difficult.

You are not a mouse

I know, I know. But similar to our rodent buddies, human pre-teens and teens find it particularly challenging to, say, plan homework schedules and suppress the urge to play video games for three hours because the brain's prefrontal cortex (where you make decisions and organize your thoughts) is still developing.

So while adults (usually) have no problem remembering to go to the store, buy milk, pick you up from school, drive you to soccer practice, and then make dinner, some kids would struggle with so many steps to deal with.

You're just a kid!

So the next time your mom gets frustrated that you forgot to take the garbage out after your piano practice,

you can tell her it's your brain's fault. It's simply struggling to place those two tasks together in sequence. (She might not buy it, but why not try?)

Read my lips

That's not the only experiment done to unlock the brain's mysteries when kids move toward adulthood. Take another well-known study conducted by a Harvard neuropsychologist (someone who studies people's behavior and how that relates to the way their brains work) a few years back. She asked teens and grown-ups to look at a bunch of photos of people's faces. Were the people in the photos...

Happy? Sad? Scared? Mad?

Here's what happened: the adults always answered correctly. The expression was fear. Yet for some reason, kids under the age of fourteen made mistakes. A lot of them thought the fearful person in the photo was angry, confused, or sad.

In other words, the kids had a tough time reading emotional signals.

NOTE TO SELF: Ask myself if my math teacher really hates me when I get an answer wrong—or if she's just in a bad mood. Maybe I'm misreading all those signals she's throwing out. Or maybe not.

What's in it for me?

Let's review the puberty brain.
Have a hard time learning new things?
Check.
Can't read facial expressions with 100 percent accuracy?
Check.
And that's just the beginning.

You see, your brain at puberty is totally geared up to search out rewards. Let's say you really want a drink of soda. Once you start craving that fizzy drink, you'll do whatever it takes to get it. Other rewards work, too. Like love. (Don't we all want some of that?) Or sleep. Or spending more time with our friends. Fair enough. Unfortunately, sometimes the rewards we crave are really unhealthy.

Before we get to what this means for you, let's just revisit our rodents for another moment...

Will work for milk

A few years back, some scientists studied our adolescent rat friends and discovered proof of this reward-craving connection. They set up an experiment that made rats of different ages push a lever to get a sip of milk.

The teenage rats? They were willing to work a lot harder to get their lactose fix than rodents of any other age. As one *Discover Magazine* article reporting on the findings put it, "They valued the milk more." That's determinaton.

Fine. Rats like milk.

What does this have to do with your non-rodent brain? A whole lot, as it turns out.

In another experiment conducted by neuroscientists (experts who study the brain), volunteers were asked to play a game while hanging out in an MRI scanner, a big machine that tracks brain activity. Once again, the volunteers were going to look at pictures of people's faces, but this time the scientists were looking for different results.

The people, ranging in age from six to twenty-nine, had to press a button every time they were shown a picture of a calm face. But they had to hold back from pressing the button when they saw a happy one.

When the researchers tallied up the results, they noticed something weird about the teens' responses. They made a lot more mistakes than the younger kids or the older adults.

(See a pattern here, yet?)

What's the pattern?

This doesn't mean that kids going through puberty are thick. But it does point to the fact that when confronted with a reward—in this case the smiley face, something that the brain thinks is awesome—teens have a harder time controlling their impulses. They like the happy face, and before they can hold back, bingo, they've pressed the button. Oops!

After analyzing the brain scans, the experts discovered that only the teens experienced a big boost to their ventral striatum, a part of the organ that has an impact on anticipation and goals. To a teen, those happy faces were extremely exciting. But what about the other part of the brain, the prefrontal cortex, which controls those responses and is supposed to stop the teens from pressing the button too soon? It grows and matures slowly.

The result? Teens' brains are stuck between two worlds. Like the rats, the teens have huge cravings for rewards, but they lack the control they need to go after them in an appropriate (read: safe) way.

Vroom, vroom

Before we get carried away, all this isn't to say that hormones don't matter. They absolutely do. Right around the time your brain is changing, the ovaries (if you're a girl) and testes (if you're a boy) empty estrogen (again, ladies) and testosterone (howdy, gents) into your bloodstream. That's your body's cue to become hairier and sprout acne. Wow! Maybe you don't agree. Moving on...

At the same time all that's happening, other sex hormones get flowing, too. Recent studies show us they affect the brain and influence things like mood and excitability. It's like they crank up the volume and leave it at eleven.

And that's where things get interesting:

Puberty brain
+ Brand-new hormones
_____
= Let's go crazy!

It's the "thrill" in thrill rides

Let's say you decide to hit your local theme park. It's got kiddy rides, games... and the biggest, baddest roller coasters around. Now take a look at who's standing in line to get on those coasters. Older people? Not many. Little kids? No way. Instead, the majority of coaster riders tend to be pre-teens, teens, and younger adults. They're totally into the rush a good 82-foot (25-meter) drop gives them. But why?

Why the rush?

Some experts think it comes down to the young brain's "need for speed." In other words, when a brain gets pummeled by hormones around puberty it grows to love that "all keyed up" feeling. It's kind of an addiction. (Remember, rats wanted the rewards more, right?) So what happens? Your brain starts sending you the signal to go out looking for situations that will give it the rush it craves.

Some of these rush-creating situations are safe. Scary movies. Eating too many Pop Rocks. Dancing like crazy. Laughing all night at a sleepover. These things can give you a boost, too.

Unfortunately, so can fast cars, drugs, and other risky behaviors that your parents are always warning you about. And when the part of your brain that throws the brakes on recklessness is still getting an overhaul? Kids keep on moving and grooving toward that rush.

You are still in control

It's not really fair to say that everything you do and everything you think can be explained away by science. There's still a lot of mystery involved when looking at why people act the way they do. Parents, friends, and siblings have a huge hand in how we all develop emotionally. So does your temperament (your natural reaction to situations). Still, it's not a bad thing to know what's going on in your body the next time you feel like throwing eggs at somebody's house with your friends. Because knowing what you know now, you can take a step back and say, "I better leave those eggs in the fridge."

After all, my brain:

- craves rewards
- has a tough time with self-control
- is just looking for its next thrill fix
- will encourage me to do riskier things when I'm around my friends

Besides, those eggs will taste better with your toast tomorrow morning. Why waste them? Delicious.

'CAUSE EVERYBODY LOOKS BETTER AFTER A LOOP-THE-LOOP

Roller coaster excitement doesn't end with gut-wrenching twists and turns. It can also make people feel a lot more, well, romantic toward complete strangers.

Back in 2008, researchers asked people to look at photos of faces before they hopped on a coaster and then again after the ride. Here's what they discovered: people who looked at the same faces afterward said the people were better looking—and they would be more willing to date them! The scientific term for this phenomenon? Roller-Coaster-Induced Excitation Transfer.

Huh.

Sure, it's easy enough to figure out when girls are hitting puberty. The clues are hard to miss. But guys? Getting a sense of when puberty starts seems a lot trickier. Or is it? Maybe not, says Joshua Goldstein, a German researcher who has been studying early puberty in boys. It turns out that boys' pubescent changes are actually pretty obvious, too—if you know what you're looking for.

In girls, the answer can be found in how early their periods start. In boys, at least according to Goldstein, the age of puberty can be traced to something called "the accident hump."

That's right. When boys reach puberty they start doing stupid things. Even risky and deadly things that land more of them in the hospital. This hazardous behavior overlaps with puberty's hormonal spikes.

By charting the number of serious accidents in boys and teens, we should be able to determine the age when they become sexually mature.

And that hump—made up of all those skateboarding-off-a-mountain-because-it-seemed-like-a-good-idea-at-the-time–type accidents—is happening earlier and earlier. Since the middle of the eighteenth century, boys have been hitting puberty about two and a half months sooner each decade.

When is it going to stop? No one is sure right now. But hopefully we can figure this conundrum out before babies start stealing the keys to take the family car out for an illegal joyride.

You're hot. (Or at least your brain is...)

As you can tell, there are a ton of child and teen brain studies and experiments being done by people all around the world. It's a pretty hot topic right now, actually. Magazines run feature articles about what's happening in that head of yours, and so do newspapers, Web sites, and radio and television shows. These studies all have the same thing in common: the potential to uncover the mystery of our behavior and feelings. Studying the brain seems to be an excellent way to get to the bottom of that. Or, at least, it's a start.

THE BIG QUESTION

When did you start to think? How do you know?

FACTS on feelings

Learn to cope. Not mope.

If you had to choose one of the following two lists of things that make us most happy, which one would you pick?

Good stuff #1

a million bucks
celebrity
a mansion and a pool
all the candy you want

Good stuff #2

creativity
ability to love and be loved
thankfulness
hope

Sure, doing laps in your own pricey pool while wolfing down jellybeans might be a lot of fun for a while, but the things you see in the second list are more likely to make you happy over the long haul. In fact, a lot of people who study something called positive psychology have discovered that people who are grateful, hopeful, and spend time with family and friends are a generally more cheerful group. Even when life throws them curveballs and bad things happen.

Get a handle on your emotions

But what happens if you don't really know how you feel? Happiness. Sadness. Anger. Worry. Everybody feels these emotions. You can think of them as a kind of clue about your thoughts.

But when people are transitioning from childhood to adulthood, their emotions become more intense—knowing exactly what is going on in your heart and head can get confusing. Of course, having that information is pretty important. After all, if you don't know what you're feeling in the first place, it's difficult to find ways to stop emotions that make you feel crummy and cause you to lash out at friends or family.

And your true inner thoughts remain mysterious...even to you.

Say hello to...
your emotional suitcase
Everybody walks around with one every day. Some days, the suitcase feels really heavy. It's full of...

 That butterflies-in-your-belly feeling? That's actually fear, an emotion that starts there and works its way up your body. Your heart races. You start to sweat. Sometimes, you'll feel the skin on your neck prickle. Some call this anxiety, but that's just a word for being afraid of something—like missing the winning shot or getting a C- in school. Fear *is* a strong emotion, but in small doses, it's a clue that something really matters to you.

 You'll sometimes feel this emotion start around your shoulder blades and move to your neck and your jaw. But your whole body can tense, too. Anger isn't all bad. It helps you say no to things that you don't want. Say something with anger, and people are more likely to listen. Problem is, we're often taught not to express it—so we stuff anger down deep inside ourselves. Soon we feel like a volcano about to erupt. Eventually we blow our top...and everybody's miserable.

SADNESS Saying good-bye to a pet for the last time. Moving away from your friends. Finding out your parents are going to get a divorce. In these moments, you'll feel a weight settle in your chest before it hits your throat and eyes. Your face feels like it's going to crumple, and you're worried you won't be able to speak. Sadness is nothing to be ashamed of. Feel it and you'll pay attention to what matters to you—whether that's visiting a sick friend or cuddling your crying baby brother.

HAPPINESS Other days, your suitcase is light.

Want to know what sadness and joy have in common? Many people say they experience them coming from the same place: the chest. Your body feels like it's filling up with about a million little pinpricks of light. Your heart swells. You smile. Everything is cool in the world. You wish this feeling would go on forever…

Most days are filled with all of these emotions. A bully is threatening you at recess. Fear. You walk away from him and your fists start to clench. Anger. The girl you've had a crush on all year slips you a note saying she wants to talk to you after school. Joy. Later that day you find out your grandma has cancer. Sadness.

This is just the way life is. Yet it's how you respond to the ups and downs that makes all the difference to how you get through puberty and grow up.

Big-time emotions

Feeling stressed? Overwhelmed? Don't know where to turn? Well, pick up a box of FeelBetter 2000. It SLICES through worries! DICES up fear! And stops anxiety COLD. Just $23.99 if you call right now. But that's not all…

Don't you wish feeling good was really that easy? But as you've probably figured out by now, life's ups and downs can make us all feel like we're along for the same hilly ride. Want proof?

The setup: It's only the second week of school, and you've already signed up for the track team and the school choir. Plus, you're still taking flute lessons and swimming. Not only are you double-booked after school, but you're worried you'll never find enough time to get your homework done. Maybe if you just crawl into bed when you get home from school and hide, it will all just go away.
The verdict: You're overwhelmed!

FOR CRYING OUT LOUD!

You've probably heard that crying can make you feel good. It calms the nerves, and you feel like a big fat weight has been lifted from your chest. Well… maybe. The truth is, experts who study sobbing and tears aren't convinced that the emotional benefits of crying are always what people think they might be.

Researchers in Florida looked at approximately 3,000 descriptions of what people felt and thought while they cried. While many volunteers certainly said they felt a lot better afterward, a number of

people did not. About a third said they could take or leave the tears. There really wasn't much of a boost. Meanwhile, one in ten of the criers said they actually felt worse.

It seems that crying is good for you only in very specific situations, such as when you've been holding your emotions in all day and need to let it all out. But crying at the wrong moment or around the wrong people? It probably won't make you feel better.

The setup: Last week, your best friend told everybody in class that you still sleep with Bunny, your favorite stuffed animal. You know that she sleeps with her dolls, but you don't say anything. Maybe you don't really want to be her friend anymore, but you feel lonely without her.

The verdict: You're hurt!

The setup: Your mom comes home from work early one day and tells you she lost her job. You can tell she's really upset but doesn't want you to know it. How are you going to get the money to buy a new backpack now that the zipper on your old one is busted? How will she pay for your apartment now? Will you have to move out?

The verdict: You're worried!

All of these situations have one thing in common—it's easy to react to them in a way that makes us feel crummy. We freeze up, cry, get angry, or even start acting crazy and silly. The main thing to remember, though, is that everybody experiences feelings they don't like. And if they're happening more often than you would like, it's okay to ask a trusted grown-up for help. Maybe some of these things on the right will help, too.

GET THAT FEEL-GOOD FEELING

Exercise. Getting outside for a run or hitting the basketball court with your friends is one of the best ways to give stress a time-out. Exercise produces endorphins, a group of hormones that can help boost your mood. This is also an easy fix if you've got the jittery, can't-sit-still feeling that's pretty common during puberty.

Talk to your friends. You don't necessarily have to have a big heart-to-heart about how procrastinating on your science project makes you feel. A simple "I've got to work on the project this weekend, or I'm going flunk it" is all it takes. You won't feel alone, and you might even decide to work together to get it done.

Create and do. Action can eliminate stress faster than anything. Take that science project—if just thinking about it stresses you out, it's time you start working on it. People often procrastinate because they can't picture the end product. Hey, who says you have to? Just pull out the pieces, or open a book to do a little research. Soon, you'll be on your way and will wonder what made you so stressed in the first place.

Be in the now. Ever realize that you usually only get stressed about things that happened in the past or might happen in the future? Take a moment. Breathe. Tell your brain to stop thinking about things you can't control. When you think about it, the present is the only reality you've got!

When the crying doesn't stop

Or the raging…or the unexplained aches and pains…there's often something deeper at work than just feeling sad or stressed out. It can be depression, and it's not always easy to spot. That's because when it comes to feeling depressed, tears aren't the only way kids express it. But here's something we do know: depression is a lot more common than most people think.

According to the World Health Organization, depression affects 121 million people worldwide.

So what exactly is depression, and how do you know if you have it? Here's what it's not: the run-of-the-mill blues. You know, that kind of gray feeling that comes over you in February when it suddenly hits you there are still four more months of school left to go? That may be not fun, but we're not talking about that.

Depression is different. It's a much stronger emotion that includes sadness, hopelessness, and despair. It can lasts weeks, months, or even years.

WHAT DOES IT FEEL LIKE?

You don't feel like doing the things that made you happy before.

You feel sad or feel hopeless—like nothing is ever going to change.

You cry a lot.

You feel restless and agitated.

You withdraw from your family and some of your friends. Going out with them doesn't seem too appealing. You'd rather stay at home and sleep.

You've got no motivation. Everything feels like a chore.

You feel like you're worthless or you're guilty of something.

You sleep and eat either more or less than usual.

You lack energy, are tired all the time, and can't concentrate.

You think about death or suicide (killing yourself).

Make sense of your symptoms

These might be some of the most common symptoms, but if you're depressed, you probably won't have all of them. You might be more irritable and angry than sad. Stomachaches, headaches, and tension are common, too. Or you might become super sensitive to any kind of criticism.

The good news is that depression can be treated with talk therapy (where you talk about your problems with a professional who can help you find ways to feel better again), as well as with medication. This is especially important if your thoughts and emotions start to spiral down, and you begin to feel really bad—bad enough to seriously harm yourself.

> **IF YOU REMEMBER ONE THING ABOUT SUICIDE, LET IT BE THIS**
>
> It's not that you want to kill yourself. It's just that you don't want to feel pain anymore. That's a completely different thing. And people can help you.

You know you're keeping your anger in when...

Some psychologists believe that anger is just a really effective way to mask sadness. So if someone doesn't feel comfortable crying or being sad, the person sometimes acts angry instead. But what happens if someone isn't down with showing or feeling that emotion either? Bottling it up only goes so far. Eventually, feelings leak out in some pretty hurtful ways and you:

- Start saying mean things about yourself. "I'm so dumb. I'm ugly. I'm weak." But these thoughts just make things worse.

- Start to hurt yourself physically.

- Take stupid risks.

- Pull away from friends and family and find yourself alone more and more.

- Overeat or stop getting exercise. All you want to do is veg.

But you can also swing too far the other way. Instead of bottling up, you:

- Destroy property.

- Say mean, hateful things about others.

- Hit or hurt other people or even pets. (This is illegal, by the way.)

- Totally freak out, even over things that seem trivial.

- Plot revenge.

If this sounds at all familiar (or you think a friend has anger issues), talk to a grown-up you trust and get help. There are also a number of organizations listed on page 97 that you can contact to make the first step toward feeling better.

How do kids and teens deal with hard times, and how can they learn new ways to feel good? These are the questions Dr. Lumley studies at University of Guelph in Canada.

"I'm really interested in learning how some kids struggle with bad life experiences and others can move forward in really positive ways," she says.

What's the secret to rolling with the punches? Well, it turns out there's no one single thing that works for everybody, but Dr. Lumley says there are a number of actions anyone can take to improve their mood. Here are a few ideas:

Accept it!

There's no rule that says we all have to feel good all the time. It's bad enough that we experience sadness or nervousness, but if we get upset and stressed about having those feelings, it only makes matters worse.

Learn to relax

When Dr. Lumley works with the kids who come to see her, she often teaches them relaxation strategies. Some people like to imagine times when they were really calm and peaceful—and then they practice feeling that way whenever they need to the most.

Take a breath

Ever notice that when you feel stressed, anxious, or upset your breathing gets wonky? Maybe you hold your breath or you take teeny-tiny ones that stay high in your chest. One way to calm down is to notice how you're breathing. "Taking a few really slow, deep breaths can make a big difference," says Dr. Lumley, who has kids blow big bubbles using bubble soap. "To get a good bubble you need to take a nice deep breath and blow out really slowly. It works!"

Calm your muscles

If breathing doesn't do it for you, learning how to relax your muscles might help. Try tensing up different parts of your body, such as your shoulders or neck, and then feel them relax again. Not sure how to do this exercise? There are tons of relaxation lessons online and on YouTube.

They won't notice

Right now there's a good chance you're starting to worry a lot more about what other kids think about you—about your clothes, your hobbies, what you say, where you live, the sports you play (or don't). Dr. Lumley says it's important to remember that most of the kids around you are thinking the same way! So relax. "Other people are a lot more focused on themselves than they are on you," she says. Maybe they're even anxious over what you're thinking about them!

Be more you

Even if you're not the best at sports or struggle in school, you've got so many amazing strengths that are important, too. Take a look at your life and notice the things that come easily to you. You're a natural-born leader? Become a camp counselor in training. A regular comedian? Learn new jokes or take an improvisation drama class. "Think about all the things that you enjoy in life—and do more of that!" says Dr. Lumley.

Use stretchy thinking!

Experts like Dr. Lumley know that what we think has a big impact on how we feel and behave. In other words, if you think, "I'm so awesome," you'll feel pretty good in general. But if you're secretly thinking, "I'm no good at anything," you'll feel sad, angry, or depressed. So learn how to get your thinking unstuck and stretch…it…out.

How?

- Let's say you think that nobody likes you.

- So you feel sad and lonely.

- But because you feel that way, you change your behavior. You go home right after school and don't talk to anybody. Or you stay inside when all the other kids on your street are hanging out together.

- You feel worse and worse!

Enter your Stretchy-Thinking Superhero! His main power? The ability to see all sides of a situation!

With his help, you realize you do have friends. (All the girls in your swimming class think your dolphin imitation is a riot, right?) Or maybe you come to understand that the boys on your street don't talk to you much because you don't talk to them! See? The more you depend on stretchy thinking, the more likely you'll feel better. Especially if you're generally a glass-half-empty, fear-the-worst kind of person.

Problematic pals

When you're on the same wavelength, good friends make life better. But sometimes, you might make a **frenemy**—an enemy disguised as a friend. Maybe you have one already. At first this friend gave your happiness a boost. Now the person is putting you down. The jabs are usually subtle, but they're definitely there. You know it because when you walk away, you always feel a bit worse than before.

- "You just started studying for the test? I started last week," he informs you. You always do well in school and don't seem to have to study as hard as everybody else, but now you're worried you'll fail.

- "I didn't know you really, really liked him," she says after agreeing to go out with a boy you've had a crush on since the beginning of the year. "You should have told me that."

Pick your enemies (and stress less)

These friends—sometimes we also call them ambivalent friends—are enough to make you feel like you're going crazy. That's not too far from the truth, actually. A number of studies show that not only do we feel more depressed if we have a lot of frenemies, but our blood pressure goes up, and we feel more stress.

What's even more interesting? When researchers studied the link between bad friends and blood pressure, they discovered that blood pressure climbs higher when we're around a frenemy than when we're around an all-out enemy, someone we really can't stand! It makes sense. We don't expect much happiness from a rival, but a bad-news friend is sure to let us down again and again. It's stressful not knowing when it's going to happen.

So why do we keep them around?

- It's in our human nature to give people the benefit of the doubt. (She was a pain today, but maybe she'll be a better friend tomorrow.)

- He's been your friend since you were in preschool, and you just can't imagine your life without him.

Definition, please
Ambivalent means having mixed feelings about something (or somebody).

- The good outweighs the bad. When your parents were getting a divorce, she was the first one to come to your house and talk about what it was like when her parents divorced. She can be a pain, but you know who to call when life gets rough.

- He's the leader of your clique, and you're too afraid to ditch him. People will sacrifice a lot (oh, say, self-esteem) to keep friends and avoid being alone. (You'll read more about this one in the next chapter.)

Am I the frenemy in this picture?

What if you're reading this and realize you're a toxic pal? Take a step back and think about why you criticize your friends, stand them up, or let them down. What are you trying to accomplish?

You've probably figured out by now that most friends behave badly because they're feeling crummy about themselves. Not only that, they're terrified that other kids will figure out they've got problems. The solution? Distraction. In other words, if you make your friends feel worse, they'll be too worried about their own issues to notice your flaws.

Sure, this theory looks all neat and clean written up on this piece of paper (or on your tablet screen, if that's how you roll), but it can't be that easy, right? It's not like you've ever actually heard yourself think, "My best friend is smarter than me, and I don't want her to know how dumb I am, so I better make her feel stupid first." Instead, you just stand her up.

Remember "stretchy thinking" a couple of pages back? That concept can apply here, too. Because your thoughts can have a big impact on how you feel, you can change your feelings if you change your thoughts. There's one really great way to get to the bottom of your thoughts: write them down. So if you know you're turning frenemy, it's a good idea to examine your thoughts to find out what's driving you. Writing it all out helps.

For example:

The situation:

My best friend, Rowan, is talking about tomorrow's math test.

How I'm feeling:

Worry. Fear. Anger.

My secret thoughts:

I'm going to fail the test! Rowan is so much better at math than me. I hate fractions. I wish I were as good as Rowan. I'm not smart at all. I don't want Rowan to know that or he won't be my friend anymore.

Once you understand the secret and under-the-surface thoughts that trigger your behavior, it's a lot easier to change them. For starters, you can use stretchy thinking and poke some holes in your beliefs about yourself. For instance:

- You've never failed a math test before. Chances are you won't fail this time.

- Rowan is really good at math, but you're really good at soccer and basketball. Plus, you got a couple of As and some Bs on your last report card. Sounds like you're sporty and smart.

- Will Rowan really dump you as a friend if you fail a test? How silly does that sound now?

You don't have to make your friends feel bad to feel better yourself. Really. Once you lighten up, pick apart your thoughts, and know you're awesome, it will be a lot easier to stick to the golden rule: treat others the way you want to be treated.

THE BIG QUESTION

Do you feel better or worse after crying? Why?

I want to fit in!

Feeling different, but wanting to be the same.

The next time you meet up with your friends, take a look at what you're all wearing. What would you see? Jeans? Skirts? T-shirts all sporting roughly the same logo? Maybe it has never occurred to you before that you're trying to look the same as the rest of the group, but there it is. The evidence is covering your chest, legs, and feet.

Clothing is just one thing people use to blend in with the crowd. It's pretty common to want to act, dress, and talk like your friends—even if, given a choice, you'd rather do something else. We call it "conformity."

Definition, please

Conformity is a change in how you behave (and even what you believe) in order to fit in with and be accepted by the larger group.

Power in numbers

There's actually a lot of good to be said about wanting to fit in. When you're at one with a group, it feels great. It feels safe. A bully's words hurt less if your friends have your back. You're stressed about a math test, until your friends admit they are, too. Feeling connected to other humans is a strong need in nearly all of us. Nothing wrong with that.

But there's a flipside. Fitting in can feel so good, we even lie or go against our own beliefs to blend in and be included.

Here, look at these lines

Want proof? Imagine you've agreed to be part of a study that you think is going to test your vision. You're put in a room and sit down at a table with five or six other people. A guy walks in carrying a stack of cards. On one, there's a line. It's about 5 inches (13 centimeters) long. There are three lines on the other card. One is the same length as the line on the first card. The other two are longer or shorter.

Your mission: say which line on the second card matches the line on the first. Easy, right? You would think. But here's

what you don't know: the rest of the participants are actors, and they've got a mission of their own—to get you to say something you don't believe.

Why would I do that?

Probably because you don't want to make waves. At first, everyone in the room gives the same answer as you, but eventually the actors all start giving the wrong (but same) answer. It's crazy! Can't they see that the lines they're choosing are completely different from the first one?

Initially, you stick to your guns and say what you think is correct. But soon, you begin to doubt yourself. Are you the one who's actually wrong? Or perhaps you begin to feel so uncomfortable being the only person to pick the right answer, you finally throw in the towel and choose the wrong one, too.

This is actually a classic experiment conducted back in the 1950s by a social psychologist named Solomon Asch. Originally, he wanted to prove that people see the world as it really is, no matter what. But the experiment showed another reality…

If the conditions are right, about two-thirds of us will eventually cave to peer pressure and say something we don't believe in.

Since then, many similar experiments have proven this point again and again.

The upside of all this

Maybe you're thinking: *No way am I going to conform and be pressured by any group. I'm going to start saying what I believe, no matter what!* Hey, we've all gotten the message that it's cool to be ourselves—it's a positive one with a lot of power. But hold on for a second. What would the world look like if everybody just did their own thing all the time? Imagine the possibilities…

- Say good-bye to group projects at school. Nobody ever agrees to anything…and that medieval poster you're all trying to draft together? It never gets done. Say hello to another "incomplete" mark.

- Elections are a nightmare! And forget about governments trying to guide a country. Nobody would be able to agree on any new laws.

- You would have arguments with your friends, parents, siblings, and teachers all the time. That much hot air isn't cool.

See? Conforming, even if that means saying something you don't actually believe just to keep the peace, isn't always a bad thing. Without some conformity and agreement, the planet would be a very chaotic, disorganized place. Having respect and learning to weigh your own beliefs and convictions against those of others is a big part of growing up. The key is having balance.

Conforming here and there by choice? Okay. Conforming so much you don't feel like yourself? It's time to speak up!

Survival of the fittest

It's amazing what we'll do just to fit in, especially when self-esteem (how confident we feel about ourselves) takes a beating. Which is exactly what can happen again and again when we hit puberty.

Especially if your friends turn on you, start gossiping and acting mean, or your emotional safety net gets pulled away.

When feet do the talking

Speaking of choices, would you eat, oh, I don't know, chicken feet if you thought it would win you friends?

A few years ago, researchers asked a group of people to take a phony personality test. When they received the results, some of them got great news—based on their answers, they could expect to be popular and happy for the rest of their lives. High-fives all around.

But for the other group? The outcomes were enough to give anyone a reason to mope. According to their results, these test subjects were headed for divorce, unhappiness, and a lifetime of loneliness.

I know, that's very mean. Thank goodness the test conclusions were bogus (and they told them so afterward!). They served their purpose, though. The whole point was to make those who got the bad news feel they were unpopular and even unlovable.

Next up, a new test. This one revolved around food. The same people were asked to write out the foods they liked versus the foods that gave them the creeps.

This brings us back to deep-fried chicken feet.

Now, there's a lot to like about the drumstick's more gristly cousin. Chicken feet are really popular in Chinese restaurants that serve dim sum, those little steamer baskets full of tasty dumplings, noodle rolls, and green veggies. The point is, however, that many people who took the survey said that chicken feet repulsed them. There was no way they'd eat them. That is, until they were matched up with a Chinese dining partner whose fave food—they were told—was chicken feet.

So what happened? Some of the people who were criticized in the first test ended up ordering the feet just to appease the person they were eating with. Why?

The thinking goes that because they now felt unsure of themselves, they were willing to go out on a limb to form a friendship, or at least to be liked. Or

to put it another way, because they'd felt excluded before, they put their best, er, foot forward and did what they had to do to become part of a group.

Enter the clique

You probably already know this term, but if you don't...

Definition, please

A clique is a group of people who like a lot of the same things or are similar in other ways. The friends in cliques spend loads of time together and—here's the important part—don't allow just anybody to join them. In short, a clique is a lot like a little exclusive family whose members choose for themselves.

Sounds pretty cozy, but the reality is anything but. That's because cliques (you can pronounce the word "kleek" or "klick," by the way—both are correct) have a dark side. In fact, they have the power to make people feel more left out, alone, and hurt than before they joined one. How? To answer that, let's take a look at how they work.

GIRLS AREN'T THE ONLY ONES WHO FORM CLIQUES

Despite how it looks on TV, boys do, too, and their cliques run the same way girls' do: by letting some boys join and leaving others out in the cold.

INSIDE THE CLIQUE

How does a clique work? Who's in?
Who's out? Should it matter to you?

Pulled in

You're drawing beside your best friend, Katie.
When you get up to go to the restroom,
another girl, Celeste, follows you in and wants
to talk. She's saying things like, "I love your hair.
You're so pretty. I wish I were as pretty as you."
Wow! You're so flattered—especially when she
asks you to sit with her in music class.

New friends

Within a few days, all of Celeste's
popular friends want you to sit
with them, eat with them, and
hang out after school. With all the
attention they're showering on
you, you feel like you belong in
their group. It's a real rush.

Cracks start to form

Soon the honeymoon is over. You
notice things you never saw before.
First off, Celeste is the boss. What she
says goes. And if you disagree with her,
she'll spread rumors about you so the
other girls will drop you. Also, your
new friends aren't being so pleasant
anymore. Sometimes they even say
things that hurt your feelings. (Like
that you're not very good-looking.)
You don't know why they put you
down, but it feels bad.

Say good-bye to your old life

The worst thing? Your clique makes fun of all the
kids who aren't in the group. Even your old best
friend, Katie. And even though you feel guilty, you
stop talking to her, too—just so Celeste won't kick
you out of the group. Because if she did, who would
you hang out with? Katie and your other old friends
are mad at you. You feel stuck.

The big picture

So why do cliques matter in the long
run? Some experts are convinced that
cliques teach kids that it's normal to
play a part in something called "group
think." That's what happens when a
whole group of people start thinking
one way because everyone else seems
to be as well. After a while, people stop
questioning what they're doing and
thinking.

In the end, cliques are all about power.
Who's in? Who's out? They're about

setting boundaries between kids who
are the same and kids who are different.
It's not the healthiest way to look at the
world, because where does it end? Is it
okay to be nasty to someone who is poor
because you have more money than the
other kid does? How about skin color or
sexual orientation? Would that keep you
from being friends? Don't forget sexism.
For ages, girls and women weren't even
considered citizens. They were less. They
were different. They weren't in.

Drawn in and cut off

Celeste might be number one in the clique, but there's a lot of jostling by the other girls to keep their power, too. Sometimes it feels like they're just looking for excuses to kick each other out. Finally they find one for you: you wore the same tights as Celeste. Stupid, right? But Celeste doesn't think so. She starts talking about you and gets everyone on her side. Nobody says it out loud, but you know you've been kicked out of the clique.

Less than zero

On a popularity scale from one to ten, you're now looking at negative numbers. Nobody sits beside you on the school bus, you can't catch anyone's eye when you have to pick science partners, and you go straight home after school and watch TV until dinner. You decide to apologize to Katie, until you notice Celeste talking to her the next day. "I love your hair. You're so pretty. I wish I were as pretty as you," you hear Celeste say…

Remember, a clique, whether it's made up of boys, girls, or both, is a group of friends, but not all groups of friends become cliques. That's because the friends within the second type of group are open to new friendships. They even encourage other kids to hang out with them because they know that new people can be a lot of fun. Cliques, however, leave other kids out on purpose. They do it to hurt.

Sometimes it turns to bullying...

Speaking of not fitting in, back in 2007, the first day of school after summer vacation started like any other at Central Kings Rural High School in Cambridge, Nova Scotia, in Canada. Students found their new lockers, talked about what they did over the break, and hit their classes.

That is, until a new ninth-grader showed up at school wearing a pink polo shirt. For that, he got razzed big-time. A bunch of older kids threatened that if he ever wore it again, he'd pay. Those were some famous last words. Soon two seniors at the school, David Shepherd and Travis Price, got wind of the bullying and hatched a plan.

They bought fifty pink shirts and sent out a message asking kids to wear them at school. Not only did those shirts get snatched up, but nearly three hundred other students showed up dressed in pink, too. It was a big moment. The bullying stopped (this was a case when conformity was a good thing!), and the media picked up the story. It went viral.

Today, schools across Canada and in other countries celebrate Pink Shirt Day at the end of February to send a message: bullying has to stop.

You know it when you see it

That's right. Bullying is a big problem. Thousands of kids every day get picked on, teased, ganged up on, beat up, insulted, and harassed because somebody decides they're "too different." In other cases, the bullying starts for what looks like no good reason at all other than that the victim seems like an easy target.

It's incredibly hurtful as well. Kids who are bullied are more likely to:

- become depressed

- refuse to go to school

- see their grades drop

- have a hard time getting to sleep

Unfortunately, it can get even worse, especially if the bullied kid can't figure out a way to get the bullying to stop. Maybe you know somebody this is happening to?

It's very sad—and frustrating— because we all have the power to make sure everybody feels safe and protected. Kids shouldn't stay up at night worrying about how to avoid using the restroom at school alone or hoping a new pair of shoes won't draw attention from the tough boys. Extreme bullying is more than stressful—it can dominate a kid's life.

Big bully picture

So why does it happen in the first place? Bullying is such a complicated issue, which is why it's so difficult to get to the bottom of it. But here are a few thoughts.

It's conformity gone bad.

As the pink shirt example shows us, sticking together can change the world, but it can also cause a lot of problems. When enough kids get together to bully another kid—their victim—that's conformity at its very worst. Being mean starts to seem like it's okay because, well, everybody else is doing it. The ugly truth is that a lot of kids get bullied because they're not playing by society's rules. They're standing out, so other kids gang up on them. Getting rid of false assumptions about what we're supposed to be like will go a long way toward stopping bad behavior.

Empathy? What empathy?

We're living in a complex world today, with the majority of people living in larger towns and cities. Some experts think that because we're starting to feel like we're just one grain of sand on the beach, we're less likely to think about people around us as other grains of sand. All we see is the big, wide beach. In other words, the people in the crowd are just faces and don't have feelings. So if you say something mean or hurt them, does it really matter? The answer is, of course it does.

Adults are still kids at heart.
Or, at least, in their heads. One of the biggest problems with bullying is that a lot of grown-ups just don't know how to handle a situation when it gets out of hand. Maybe they were bullied, too, when they were kids, and it still stresses them out. Or even worse, they wind up blaming the victim because they buy into society's stereotypes and biases, such as thinking that boys should "act like men" and be tough. Still, there are also a lot of adults who see bullying for what it is and will have your back. So if the first person you talk to isn't helping you, find someone who will.

HOW TO ACT IN THE MOMENT

If other kids are giving you a hard time, it's probably going to make you angry. But don't fight back, because that usually makes the situation worse, says Rob Frenette, an anti-bullying activist in Canada. "Two wrongs don't make a right, and giving back aggressively is not going to help your situation in any way," he says. A lot of bullies just want to see you react because it makes them feel like they've got power over you. Don't give them the satisfaction. Instead, Rob has a few ideas that might help.

The next time someone is in your face

• Walk away or ignore what the bullies are doing.

• Say something complimentary to the bully to distract him or her.

• Stay in a group (bullies are less likely to pick you out if you're with other people).

• Tell someone you trust about it afterward.

If you witness a bully in the act

• Run and get help from an adult.

• Stand beside the kid who is being verbally hurt.

• Say "stop."

• Lead the victim away from the situation.

• Get to know the victim.

Remember, if you're being bullied, it's not your fault. You're not weak or unlikeable just because someone else doesn't know how to treat people properly. Bullies lash out because they have problems of their own, not because of anything you've done or anything you are.

Are you the bully here?

Nobody wants to think they're a bully. After all, "bully" is a pretty loaded word, and you're certain that the way you treat other kids wouldn't fall into that category. You don't punch anybody or take their lunch money, right? Still, when all your friends are yelling at other kids, sometimes you join in. Or maybe you put down another girl's clothes because you want to see how she'll react. Cry? Get mad?

The thing about bullying is that it has a habit of shifting around. One moment you're being bullied and a couple of weeks later you might find yourself bullying somebody else. Relationships are complicated because everybody's bringing their own problems to each situation.

- **Your parents** yell at you all the time, and you think that's just normal.

- **You're afraid** that if you don't bully, everybody else will think you're weak and bully you. You want control over your own life.

- **Bullying gives you status**, power, and popularity. (And you really want that stuff!)

- **Someone you like is encouraging** you to be mean, and you don't know how to say no.

- **Something bad is happening** in your life right now—you just moved or there's a death in your family—and you feel angry. So you lash out at anyone who will let you get away with it.

- **You just feel all-around bad** about yourself and think you're kind of a failure.

JUST BECAUSE IT'S ONLINE...

Doesn't make bullying any less wrong. Or less harmful. Cyberbullying—when a child or teen is harassed, tormented, teased, threatened, or targeted by another one using the internet—still hurts. Cyberbullies might send hurtful messages directly to the victim, post nasty stuff for everyone to see, or even send computer viruses. Even worse, they can do a lot of damage by pretending they're the victim and writing hateful things online.

There are a few things you can do to keep yourself from being cyber-burned. For starters, keep your instant message, Facebook, and phone accounts safe. Never share that information with anyone you don't trust. It's also important to google yourself from time to time just to see what's being written about you.

Bullies aren't actually that strong

Bullies and clique leaders don't have an easy time, even though it might look that way from the outside. The reality is, some kids are dealing with a lot of pent-up anger and worry because of things that are going on at home or because they feel like they don't measure up at school. Maybe they feel like they don't have friends they can trust. So one way for them to feel better? Make someone else feel even worse. If you've been having the urge to hurt other kids, either through fists or words, go to a teacher, parent, favorite uncle, or school counselor and talk about what's going on with you. It might feel weird at first, but you've got the right to be happy, too.

A few good friends

Finally, here's some good news: it's actually not necessary to have loads of friends to feel liked and accepted. Ranking up there on the popularity scale doesn't do much for happiness either.

So what's the secret to being true to yourself and happier no matter where you land in the popularity pecking order?

- A couple of close friends are better than two hundred Facebook friends. They're the real deal.

- Studies show that even if you just think you're liked and feel comfortable around people, it goes a long way socially. Stay positive.

- Know that things will change. Even if you don't feel like you fit in now (and yes, it feels uncomfortable and hurts), eventually you'll find other people who will get your jokes, wear similar clothes, or listen to the same music you do.

THE BIG QUESTION

Would you lie about something to fit in at school? How about cheat, gossip, or steal? How far would you go to make friends?

I've got a crush on you...

New feelings about other people are exciting, scary, and fun.

It's amazing how little shut-eye you've been getting lately. Sure, you stumble into bed each night after going through your teeth-brush, wash-face routine. But the moment you close your eyes? A specific person's face pops into your head, and it's hard to get to sleep.

You imagine new and different ways you'll be able to bump into him tomorrow between classes.

Or you start to worry about that new big pimple on your chin and wonder if she'll notice it, too.

Does this behavior actually point to some kind of obsession? It sure feels that way. But the reality is that when you hit puberty and hormones kick in, you start to see certain people in a new light. And sometimes those feelings for one person grow and grow some more.

Looking for like-like

When you were a little kid, a close grown-up's affection was enough to keep you happy. But now that you're hitting puberty, your body is telling you it's time to branch out and find other sources of love and affection beyond your family ties. This is great. Forming strong relationships is part of growing up—although you're probably going to be in for a ride because things can get complicated once you throw emotions and romantic attraction into the mix.

That's why when you like another person a lot—and feel a bit nervous, hot, sweaty, and excited whenever he or she is around—we call that a crush. A crush isn't always easy to deal with because it can create so many conflicting emotions.

- You really want to get close and talk to the person. You also want to run and hide when he or she is near.

- You wonder what would happen if the person feels the same way about you. You totally freak out about how you might react if that's the case.

Confusing stuff. Even more confusing? A lot of girls think boys don't feel the same way about crushes as they do.

"He only wants one thing."

OR **"He doesn't like me because he's always making fun of me."**

Meanwhile, a lot of boys assume girls are on a different planet entirely when it comes to feeling the crush.

"She doesn't like me because she never says anything to me."

OR **"If I act really cool and distant, she'll like me more."**

With so many assumptions and mixed messages, it's no wonder a lot of kids experiencing their first crush make a few mistakes. Maybe your crush shows interest in you, but you freeze and can hardly say anything. Or worse, you panic and say something kind of mean. It can be incredibly difficult to talk about how you really feel.

But here's the good news about crushes: they're just the first step toward having a girlfriend or boyfriend someday. If you don't get it right today, you can always try again tomorrow and the day, month, or year after that. There's plenty of time.

You might even want to think of crushes as a safe zone. You can feel all the fun emotions of falling in love, but without having to get yourself into situations you might not be ready for. In other words, there's a reason why all the other girls in your class are going crazy about the latest celebrity heartthrob. He's the ultimate safe and fun fantasy boyfriend.

But nobody likes me!

Give it time. According to a study in the United States, by the time Americans are eighteen, about 80 percent of them have had at least one important romantic relationship. As for grown-ups, up to 75 percent of them eventually marry. Not that you have to get married if you don't feel like it (or have to make up your mind right now!), but if that's what you want, the odds are in your favor.

IS THIS WHAT A CRUSH FEELS LIKE?

Everybody keeps talking about who has a crush at school right now. But when it comes to your own feelings, you're in the dark. How would you ever know you have a crush?

You think about one person more than anyone else.
He's always on your mind, and you can't stop thinking about what he looks like, how he talks, and when you'll see him again.

You feel excited and happy.
Or maybe you feel more hyped up than usual and don't feel like eating or sleeping. Most of the time, though, you feel like there's a light growing in your chest and making your days feel so much more fun—even when your crush isn't around!

You can't concentrate.
Having a hard time sticking to your homework schedule? Feel your brain drifting off because you just want to dream about the person you have a crush on? That shiver of excitement isn't going away.

You think about how you look and act.
Especially when you're around the person you like. And if she's not around? You're still thinking about it—even if it's just hovering around at the back of your mind.

You go out of your way to see your crush.
Do you have to pass by your crush in the hall on the way to class? You'll probably make sure you're there on time to catch a glimpse or have a quick chat.

You talk about your crush...a lot.
And now your friends are rolling their eyes every time you bring him up. Or you slip her name into conversations, without being quite so upfront about your feelings.

You talk to a fortune teller to find out if you and your crush have a future.
Ha. Just kidding. Kind of. Crushes make us do all kinds of crazy things that wouldn't have made any sense at all only a few months ago.

Love, lust, or something else?

You know the phrase, "love at first sight"? It's kind of a lie. In reality, romantic feelings change over time. And they rarely start with honest-to-goodness love. Instead, according to Helen Fisher, a biological anthropologist, Rutgers University professor, and scientific adviser to a dating site called Chemistry.com, romantic feelings follow a specific pattern that starts at one place and ends somewhere else entirely. The path looks something like this...

Point A: The crush!

Actually, Professor Fisher calls this feeling "lust," but no matter what name it goes by, it's about being totally into the way someone looks and their body. You'll have a zingy feeling when the person is near—even if you've never spoken to him or her in your life! (By the way, sometimes this is where the story ends. A lot of first fixations never get past this stage, and that's okay! Crushes are fun, and you're learning a lot about what kind of person you really, really like.)

Point B: Love struck...Bingo

You're going out, and it's going swell. You might even want to call this the magnetism phase because this is when people feel drawn to each other like magnets! The girl of your dreams? The feelings you have for her are bigger and more important than anyone else's on the planet. The love of your life? He can do no wrong, and if he has flaws, you think they're incredibly cute and special. You feel amazing when the relationship is going well...but there can also be terrible mood swings when it's not.

Point C: The bond

This is the big prize. Once you get here with your partner, you feel a sense of peace and calm. It's about stability and building a future together.

HERE, SMELL THIS

Speaking of attraction, could our noses have something to do with who we're initially into? Maybe.

Years ago, a zoologist in Switzerland asked forty-nine men to wear a new T-shirt to bed for two days. To be sure their human scent wasn't contaminated, he also doled out unscented soap. Soon after the guys dropped off their shirts, women were brought in to sniff them and rate which ones they liked. (Let's hope they were also given clean shirts that read, "I SURVIVED THE SWEATY T-SHIRT STUDY OF 1995!")

The outcome was pretty bizarre. Far more women said they preferred the smell of T-shirts worn by men whose immune response genes were different from their own. Huh? Well, to put it simply, their genes were compatible for making the healthiest kids. Scientists already knew that mice have the gift of sniff, but this was one of the first times there was proof that humans do, too.

Crush or obsession?

Crushes are normal, but are you having a normal crush? Here are a few signs you're merging onto the road of an unhealthy obsession:

- Staring at your crush all the time... and making the person feel super-uncomfortable.

- Continuing to ask her to hang with you, even though she has told you she doesn't want to—more than once.

- Calling, emailing, texting, or IMing him even when he doesn't respond.

- Feeling really depressed and upset because he doesn't feel the same way you do.

- Getting angry and wanting to lash out at the person.

ONE LOOK, YOU WERE HOOKED

And now you can't stop thinking about how loved you'd be if only you could snag...the latest techno gadget. Let's face it. We don't just experience the sweaty-palm, racing-heart emotions when we come face to face with a person.

Person crush—you think about him or her all the time, spend hours daydreaming about your time together, feel overwhelming desire...

Thing crush—you think about it all the time, spend hours daydreaming about your time together, feel overwhelming desire...

Sound familiar? Crushes are all about fantasy— no matter what it is you're interested in!

If you think you might be obsessed, talk to a friend, sibling, or parent. Sometimes just talking about the problem will help you cope and get a grip. But if you don't feel comfortable with that, it's helpful to remember that obsessions are pretty unhealthy. They can make you do things that upset and even scare the person you have strong feelings for. Add that to the fact that obsessing can make you feel unhappy and out of control, and it's easy to see why it's time to stop.

The games we play

Okay, say you have a crush on someone, but they don't seem to know you exist. What are you supposed to do? Send smoke signals? Sing a midnight serenade? Actually, there's something else most people try first that's a little less dramatic.

Flirting is a basic instinct that most humans share. It's part of our nature and one of the first steps to making a romantic connection. But exactly how common is it? Back in 2004, the Social Issues Research Centre in Oxford, United Kingdom, asked a thousand young people to discuss how often they flirt.

- 99 percent admitted to at least some flirting in their lifetime.

- Over a third said they'd flirted with someone either "today" or "within the past week."

It's a universal language, too. The same moves have been documented everywhere from within African tribal villages to New York City. Obviously, much of flirting is actually about body language:

- intense eye contact
- smiling
- syncing up body movements
- touching your own hair
- head tilting in girls
- chest thrusting in guys

Later on, it can look a lot more like this:

- winking
- laughing or giggling
- flattery
- teasing
- sending notes or IMs
- finding ways to "bump into" the person

Hey, she started it!

That might not be too far from the truth, actually. Researchers have found that two-thirds of what they call "flirtation sequences" are started by girls and women.

Except guys aren't necessarily good at noticing when they're being flirted with! Not consciously anyway. In one study, men were asked to describe flirting scenes between men and women after they happened. Nearly every volunteer talked about what the guys were doing at the beginning of the exchange, but only three described how the women flirted. Yet, without saying a word, the women had been sending up to fifty-two different clues that they were interested.

JUST DO IT

The moment of truth. You want to take flirting to the next level. Worried you'll be rejected? That's natural. But if you don't ask, you'll never find out if the person is into you.

There's a chance you won't be turned down anyway. There's even scientific proof. Back in 2010, some research assistants (students who help out their professors) walked up to complete strangers on the street and said, "Hi, my name is Nate (or Abby, or whatever). I am sorry to disturb you like this, but I have been noticing you around and find you very attractive. Would you go on a date with me tonight or during the week/weekend?"

Seriously. Strangers. On the street. With that line.

Now, there wasn't anything super amazing about these volunteers either. They were average-looking, just like most of the people we know. Even so, of all the single people they asked...

- 68 percent of guys agreed to the date
- 43 percent of the women gave the idea a thumbs-up

Another similar study from the past pegged it at more of a fifty-fifty split.

So just to make it clear: if an average-looking person can convince a complete stranger to go out with him or her (with a lame opening line, no less), what's holding you back from asking out the cutie who keeps shooting you "the look" when you pass in the hall?

Suddenly your odds are looking a lot better, aren't they?

How to play

Wow. Flirting, crushes, and attraction can be confusing. Or are they? Grab a set of dice and find out.

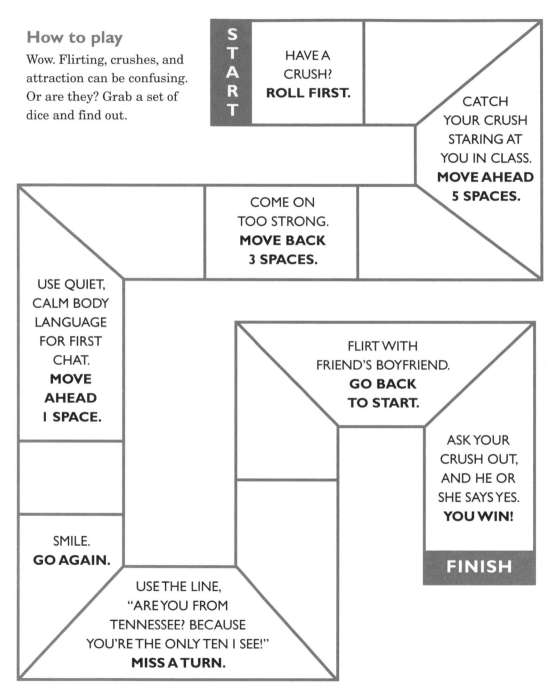

START

HAVE A CRUSH? **ROLL FIRST.**

CATCH YOUR CRUSH STARING AT YOU IN CLASS. **MOVE AHEAD 5 SPACES.**

COME ON TOO STRONG. **MOVE BACK 3 SPACES.**

USE QUIET, CALM BODY LANGUAGE FOR FIRST CHAT. **MOVE AHEAD 1 SPACE.**

FLIRT WITH FRIEND'S BOYFRIEND. **GO BACK TO START.**

ASK YOUR CRUSH OUT, AND HE OR SHE SAYS YES. **YOU WIN!**

SMILE. **GO AGAIN.**

USE THE LINE, "ARE YOU FROM TENNESSEE? BECAUSE YOU'RE THE ONLY TEN I SEE!" **MISS A TURN.**

FINISH

Desperate to connect

Okay. Let's get this straight. You're pretty sure your crush is into you. The person is throwing out all the signals. The smiles. The head tilt. The whole bit. Only one problem: you've never actually spoken to each other. Well, not since second grade anyway. So how are you supposed to make your move—especially if you're shy?

Shyness isn't the same thing as being introverted—someone who feels comfortable with and even energized by alone time. Shy people desperately want to reach out to people, but they don't know how. Or they feel uncomfortable in social situations.

To the rest of the world, you just look standoffish or quiet. But inside, your emotions are anything but. Everything feels like it's on red alert! You might even feel sick to your stomach or experience a headache coming on.

The problem with shyness is that it can have a big impact on your life because you end up holding back from what you would like to do.

Maybe you're not actually shy

Instead, you're simply experiencing run-of-the-mill nervousness about approaching the person you like. That's normal, really. How do you overcome it? Think small. As in, find a way to make small talk about something you know you both have in common. A teacher. A history project. A club you're both a part of. This conversation does not have to be the be-all and end-all of you and a crush moving forward. It's just a start.

Remember, you might think this is the person of your dreams, but you honestly don't know if that's true. Opening your mouth is also about you figuring out who you want to spend time with. Keep that in mind and the start of any relationship becomes a whole lot easier.

THE BIG QUESTION

In your mind, what's the difference between liking somebody and like-liking them?

The G word

Gay, straight, lesbian, bisexual, or transgender. We are who we are!

You're walking down the hall, minding your own business, when some kid you barely know bumps into you and says something along the lines of "Watch it, gay boy," or "What's your problem, lesbian?" You know this person was trying to be hurtful, but seriously? Gay boy? Lesbian? What's that about?

Well, in a very hurtful way, he's talking about homosexuality. You've probably heard the word before. Perhaps you know it very well. Your favorite uncle is gay or transgender, or you have two moms. Or maybe you're starting to suspect it applies to you now that you're having these new more-than-a-friend feelings for someone who is the same sex as you.

The weird thing about homosexuality is that it can get some people seriously riled up. And if you're starting to feel romantic about other people, there's a chance that homosexuality, or being gay, is on your mind. At first, figuring out who you are attracted to can lead to a lot more questions than answers.

KNOW THE TERMS

- **Homosexual**
  Being attracted to people who are the same sex as you.

- **Gay**
  Boys who are attracted to boys; men who are attracted to men. This is also used as a catchall phrase for being homosexual.

- **Lesbian**
  Girls who are attracted to girls; women who are attracted to women.

- **Bisexual**
  People who are attracted to both men and women.

- **Transgender**
  Those who feel they're a different gender than the one they were born as. So a boy feels like he's really a girl. Or a girl sees herself as a boy.

- **Straight**
  Girls who like boys, and boys who like girls.

LGBTQ? That's lesbian, gay, bisexual, transgender, and queer (or questioning), just so you know. There's no one right way to be straight, gay, or bi. Everybody has his or her own unique story.

A squiggly line?

Discovering whether you will eventually be attracted only to boys, to girls, or even to both can take a bit of time. Or not.

- Some people say they've always known that they were straight, gay, or lesbian.

- Others tell another story and explain they thought they were straight for a long time, but realized they were gay or lesbian later.

- Some teens try kissing, hugging, and exploring with others who are the same sex. They might wonder if they're homosexual, but eventually feel most comfortable in straight relationships as they grow up.

It can take time

In fact, it's normal for pre-teens and teens to have crushes and sexual feelings for other kids who are the same sex and people of the opposite sex, too. Sometimes these feelings are a clue about who they'll eventually become as an adult. But not always.

Sexual orientation—the term that we use to describe a pattern of who we're most often attracted to—isn't always a straight line or a quick process. In the end, only time will tell whom you'll eventually love.

THE TALK

WITH STEVEN SOLOMON, SCHOOL SOCIAL WORKER FOR THE TRIANGLE PROGRAM —a high school program for LGBTQ youth in Toronto, Canada

During the past fifteen years that Steve has been talking to kids and teens about homosexuality, he has been asked a lot of questions about what it means to be gay, lesbian, bisexual, or transgender. Here are a few that come up most often.

Q: When does someone choose to be gay?

A: Sometimes it's helpful to flip this one around. How old is a straight person when they know they're straight? People realize that they're straight or gay at generally the same time. The difference is that if someone is gay and wants to come out, there is going to be a real possibility of getting some negative reactions. So they hold on to that personal information for a while.

Q: My friend just told me she's a lesbian. What should I say?

A: When a friend comes out to you, there are two words you should say immediately: "Thank you. Thank you for trusting me with this." Also remember that when your friend comes out to you, it's not the same as coming on to you! That's a myth.

Q: I feel so alone with my feelings and really want to tell someone what's going on in my heart. What should I do?

A: Turn to a trusted adult in your life. It doesn't have to be your parents or an adult in your home. It could be a teacher, a family friend, or a counselor. There are so many great resources online, too. I really like PFLAG, or Parents, Families and Friends of Lesbians and Gays. It has solid information for kids and their parents, too. Or call a help line. There are people there who will listen.

TRAPPED!

How would you feel if you went to sleep as a girl last night and woke up this morning with a boy's body? Confused and a little freaked out, right? Well, that's generally how transgender kids feel, although the feeling usually builds over time. While we use the term "sexual orientation" to describe whom we're attracted to, "gender identity" covers how we see ourselves.

This is how Steven Solomon puts it:

"I was born a guy; I like being a guy, and I feel like a guy. So my gender identity is male. But as some people grow up, they realize their feelings on the inside don't match their body on the outside. We might use the word 'transgender' because the gender they feel like is not the gender that people see. Some kids even say they were born into the wrong body."

Because many kids figure out their gender identity early, some parents are doing what they can to help their transgender children get through puberty without so much anxiety. There are a number of recent cases in which parents, with a doctor's support, have given their kids special medications to slow puberty down. For a girl who feels like a boy inside, getting a period or growing breasts can be confusing and upsetting. Putting it off for a few more years can make a big difference emotionally.

WHY SAYING "THAT'S SO GAY" HURTS

It seems innocent enough. You're hanging around with your buddies playing the latest shoot-'em-up video game when one of you says, "Get out of my way, homo, or you're going to get shot." Or maybe your best friend just got a test score back, takes one look at her bad mark, and says, "That's so gay."

Even if these remarks seem harmless, you might not realize how hurtful they can be to someone who's gay or is close to someone who is. When people throw around words like "gay" or "homo," it automatically suggests to everybody in the room that being gay is a really bad thing. Think stupid and worthless.

Look at it this way. Let's say your name is Abby. Up until now you've always liked your name. That is, until some kids start using it as a slur. Suddenly everybody's saying things like, "Dude, your sweater is so Abby!" Or, "Did you see the awful episode last night? Wasn't that Abby?"

How would you feel about who you are? What if your little sister's name was Abby? Think about it.

ALL TOGETHER NOW

In Canada, nearly 10 percent of straight students have received homophobic insults or even been beat up because people thought they were gay. Why not start a Gay–Straight Alliance club at your school? You can help make school safe for everyone, gay and straight.

So why the bullying and fear?

That's a good question. Although it doesn't make a lot of sense to make people feel bad about who they choose to love or who they feel they are inside, homosexuality and transgender can be a touchy subject.

Some people say that their religious books say these ways of living are wrong—although other similar religions welcome everybody into their churches or temples no matter who they like. In dozens of countries, homosexuality is still against the law, although that's changing in some places around the world.

Family has a lot to do with how we feel about other people, too. If Mom and Dad say homosexuality is wrong, it might take a long time for their children to come up with their own ideas and decide that being gay is no big deal. For others, though, homosexuality simply makes them feel uncomfortable because they don't have a lot of experience with gay people. It seems unfamiliar and even a little scary.

And don't forget gender stereotypes. To someone who is used to thinking that boys = blue and girls = pink, homosexuality seems to break all the rules about how people are supposed to behave, at least according to how things used to be. How can a guy be a real guy if he's into other guys? A girl who loves another girl? That doesn't seem natural because aren't all girls supposed to want boys to be attracted to them? Hey, that's what all those princess movies we grow up with seem to tell us. Talk about messing around with some people's view of the world!

No matter why people come down hard on homosexuality, though, it doesn't make it right. Every person has the right to love and live without put-downs and fear.

In the halls at school

Homosexuality leads to a lot of big questions. Throw sex into the mix— something that many cultures in the world have trouble discussing, especially with kids—and suddenly you've got a perfect storm of anxiety.

In North America, attitudes toward homosexuality are changing as it becomes much more accepted in society and the media. See enough boys or men holding hands on TV and eventually it's not much of a big deal, even if that's not what you're into. But the problem is that in real life, in real school hallways, there's still a lot of homophobia. Even as characters on, say, the TV show *Glee* come out and are loved for who they are, many more kids at actual schools are teased and harassed.

No wonder kids and teens who are gay or transgender (or who think they might be) have such a tough time during puberty. It's incredibly easy to feel out of sync with your friends if most of them want to talk up the hot girl during lunch break and you're not interested in the slightest. It's even tougher if other kids call you names or bully you in other ways because they think you don't act as masculine as you should, or think you should date boys when you like girls.

I didn't think he was serious...

Kids who are bullied are more likely to think about suicide than those who aren't. And LGBTQ victims of homophobic bullying are even more likely to consider suicide. After all, it's much harder to get help from an adult when you're afraid that reporting the bullying will "out" you.

Not that the bullying is always done out in the open, although sometimes it is, especially if it turns into punching,

WHAT'S HOMOPHOBIA?

It's the hatred or fear of people who are homosexual. Sometimes it leads to saying mean and hostile things to someone else to make them feel bad, and occasionally it results in acts of violence. In other cases, people who are homophobic aren't so upfront about their feelings. They might give a job to someone who they think is straight instead of someone who they think is gay. Or a homophobic teacher might not step in when other kids are bullying a gay student.

If you're gay and kids are being nasty to you, try to remember one thing: there's nothing wrong with you. Homophobia is the problem.

hitting, kicking, or destroying belongings. But many times homophobic bullying is done in secret. Whispered rumors. Being excluded from things like parties or hanging out after school with friends.

Gay or straight, there are usually signs that someone you know is thinking about committing suicide.

- He says things like, "I'd be better off dead," or "They'd be sorry if I died."

- She has a lot of mishaps, like broken bones or falling down stairs. You start to wonder if she wants to hurt herself.

- He's giving away his things (even the stuff you know he loves).

- He says good-bye in a way that's out of character, like hugging you when he normally wouldn't.

- You've caught her asking about pills, weapons, or other ways to kill herself.

Of course it's a risk

Not everybody is going to be this transparent. So you've got to trust your gut. If you have a niggling suspicion that when someone you know says bye, it means a lot more, tell a grown-up fast. Your teacher. Your parent. His parents. Her older sister. Just do it. If it turns out your friend was just kidding around, he or she will get over being angry eventually. But if you were right, you'll be saving a life.

GET INVOLVED, JUST LIKE...

Ben Cohen, a world-class English rugby star, is now dedicating his life to eradicating bullying and homophobia in sports. A lot of people ask him if he's gay. He's not. He just thinks it's time to treat everybody with respect. The You Can Play program—a gay–straight athletes' alliance that features the support of many professionals from the National Hockey League—is based on the same idea.

"It's important for straight athletes at all levels to step up and let gay athletes know they will be accepted, and to let other straight athletes know that homophobic language and attitudes are never appropriate," said Brian Burke, the former general manager of the Toronto Maple Leafs who helped get the program going along with his son, Patrick.

Gay, straight, transgendered, it doesn't matter. We all have the right to be who we are. Kicking a ball or shooting a puck for a living shouldn't change that.

Why not take a page from Ben, Brian, and Patrick's book?

THE BIG QUESTION

If a boy likes another boy, does that mean he's gay? If a girl likes another girl, is she a lesbian? Why?

CHAPTER 9
Relationships

Getting it right

Psst! Here's the secret to love: keep it real.

First base. Second base. Third base. Isn't it funny how we use baseball terms to describe what happens when relationships turn romantic and we start thinking about exploring our sexual side? It says a lot about how we view these connections in the first place: relationships = playing games.

- The person you're supposed to really like, or even love, is on one team.

- You're on the other.

- And the whole thing turns into a competition.

How exactly is this healthy? No wonder so many new relationships have a hard time taking off...or blow up after a couple of days, weeks, or months. Healthy and

78

happy relationships aren't about winning and losing. Or about who gets their way and who has to give in.

The real deal

In a strong relationship, games get the big strike out. It's about being honest about who you are, what you think, and what you like. It's about talking about stuff that matters to you. It's about listening, sharing, giving respect, and expecting respect in return.

So what does a healthy relationship actually look like?

☑ **Like this.**

You're going out with a girl, and you're totally into her. When she's around, you feel like you can say anything, and she understands where you're coming from. She doesn't care who your friends are or what clothes you wear. She just loves the person you are inside, and that feels great.

☑ **Like this.**

You think his bad jokes are cute, and when he was really upset after his hockey team lost the important game, you wanted to make him feel better.

☒ **Not this.**

You make out with your boyfriend all the time, but really, you find him kind of annoying. Plus, it embarrasses you when he wears that purple shirt that you know he likes but you think makes him look geeky.

☒ **Not this.**

You've been going out for a few weeks now and she's ready to go further sexually than you are. How can you say no? Isn't that what all boys want?

Will work for skills

Early on, it's normal to think your boyfriend or girlfriend is the best thing. After all, if you've been waiting to be part of a couple for what feels like ages, there's a good chance you'll be totally psyched by the whole idea of being with someone. How do you know if it's "love"? That takes time to develop and is different for everyone, but here are some things to look for.

Respect. Actually, make that mutual respect. He gets how amazing you really are, and you don't feel the need to change anything about him. Hey, there's a reason you decided to be together, right? It wasn't because you wanted to use up all those 2-for-1 hamburger coupons. It was because you loved his wicked sense of humor and kindness. Meanwhile, he loved that when you smiled at him, you really meant it.

I'M NOT READY FOR THIS!

Not interested in a relationship just yet? No worries! But don't skip this chapter. You'd be surprised how many lessons here will relate to your other friendships, too.

Listening skills. This fits in with respect, actually. Do you try to push each other's boundaries? If you say you don't want to go any further sexually, does he listen? If you know her parents are strict about her curfew, do you try to get her to stay at your house just a little later, even when she protests? Good relationships are about listening, understanding, and playing by the rules.

Honesty and trust. You can't have one without the other. If you're honest about your feelings and what you both need, trust just happens. You tell your honey that you weren't staring at the cute new kid in school, and he or she believes you. End of story. Trust can be a tough one if it has been broken before, though. Maybe you told him you couldn't hang out after school because you had to study but went to the mall with your friends instead. If he finds out, it's time to be honest and tell him why.

Just be you. Talk about exciting. Here you are, part of a couple, and everybody is starting to see you that way. Well, hold on. Is that what you really want? The best relationships are the ones where two people are in them, but they both keep some independence. You have your families, your friends, and your hobbies. You don't drop them to be with your new flame. You should be free to make friends, take on hobbies, and stretch your wings—all while having a relationship.

Support. It's nice to have someone to hug you if you've had a bad day or you find out you didn't make the team. This support might be even more important to you if you are gay and feel you have to keep your true sexual feelings hidden from everyone but your girlfriend or boyfriend. That person might be the only one you feel comfortable and safe talking to about what you're going through.

Don't go too crazy trying to figure out whether what you've got is love. You're young! Enjoy being around someone you dig.

Hold (too) tight

For many people, all of this stuff is a no-brainer. After all, everyone looks for the same thing in their relationships, no matter if they're straight, gay, lesbian, bi, or transgender: someone who loves them, is supportive, and respects them.

Only one problem: we don't always choose the best people for us. Sometimes we stay with people who are a bad choice for far too long.

Especially when dating is new, you might be so excited to go out with someone that you don't really care who it is! It's a big self-esteem booster to know that another girl or boy is into you. But once you realize you don't have much in common or the other person isn't nice to you, you both lose interest and the relationship stops.

It's okay to be alone

However, some people hold on to a relationship for too long because they're scared to be alone, or they like everybody knowing they have a boyfriend or girlfriend. Or they feel bad about themselves and say, "Who else would want me?" A bad relationship can also turn into a habit. It might not make you feel good, but at least you know what to expect. Just remember that "familiar" isn't the same thing as "good." So even if it feels scary, getting out of a bad or simply boring relationship makes sense.

Crossed signals

Building a caring relationship with someone you trust isn't easy at first. There are so many forces that work against it. Take the media.

GIRLS ARE TOLD...
• Wear makeup and look beautiful at all times. It also helps not to say a whole lot.
• And those boys? They only want one thing (it starts with an S and ends with E-X).

BOYS ARE TOLD...
• Love makes you weak.
• Don't get too wrapped up in a relationship because girls will weigh you down.

These stereotypes are everywhere. Girls' magazines. TV. In the locker room. But the real truth? For the majority of boys and girls, these weird ideas don't gel with how they truly feel at all.

JUST BECAUSE YOU HAVE AN ARGUMENT

It doesn't mean you have to break up. Disagreements are part of good relationships and are nearly inevitable. You have your opinion and your boyfriend or girlfriend has one, too. That's what you liked about him or her in the first place, right? So if nearly every couple disagrees from time to time, why do some of those conversations turn so sour they lead to breaking up? The trick is to keep arguments clean. So no name calling, put-downs, or threats if you want your relationship to last. Instead: SPEAK. LISTEN. REPEAT.

MIXED MESSAGES are MIXED UP

"We have this whole culture of masculinity—characteristics and behaviors that boys are supposed to embody. You're supposed to be strong and unemotional. You're supposed to be very intelligent, and eventually you're going to make a lot of money so you can be the breadwinner.

At the same time, there's increasing pressure on young men to be emotional and be a good boyfriend. You're getting mixed messages and don't really know how you're supposed to behave."

—*Tracy Penny Light, a Sexuality, Marriage, and Family Studies/History professor from St. Jerome's University in Waterloo, Canada.*

SAY NO TO PIGEONHOLES

When it comes to gender, there are a ton of stereotypes: Girls who don't want to have sex are prudes. (Nope. They just don't want to have sex.) Or boys are supposed to be strong and never cry. (Wrong again.)

Those are obvious ones, and they can lead to breaking up if people buy into the lies. But there are other more subtle stereotypes that can do a number on a relationship and turn it inside out. Call them the Reality Swipers.

Imagine you're a girl and you're taking your boyfriend out for lunch. Maybe you're thinking: "Wow! I love this restaurant. It makes the best Pad Thai. I'm so happy I can take Aiden here. In fact, today it's my treat. I have enough cash for both of us."

No problem, right? But perhaps this is what Aiden thinks when the bill comes: "Wow! Love this place. My girlfriend is right, it has the best Pad Thai ever. But wait…why is she paying for my part of the meal? I'm the guy here. I'm not supposed to let her pay. This is making me feel kind of guilty."

Okay, maybe Aiden didn't think those exact words, but because society still has some tired, old hang-ups about how boys and girls should act—such as who pays for what—having his meal paid for can feel strange. He might even get resentful, and the next thing you know, two days later he's telling you he's feeling smothered and needs a break. All because of someone paying for noodles!

If you ever feel odd about doing something just because it's what you heard boys or girls are supposed to do, talk about it. Your partner likely thinks the stereotype is just as silly as you do!

Hey boys! The pressure's on

Let's take a look at one more stereotype—say you've taken the leap and now you've got a relationship going. This is a big step. But here's another one: how far will you go?

The way the rest of the boys talk at school, you'd think they were all hooking up all the time. Not so fast. A few years ago, the popular girls' magazine *Seventeen* conducted a survey of twelve thousand boys and young men aged fifteen to twenty-two. Here's a sample of the results:

- 60 percent said they had lied about something sexual
- 30 percent said they had lied about "how far they had gone"
- 78 percent said they felt there was too much pressure to have sex

So girls aren't the only ones to feel the heat. Other research indicates that one in three boys say they feel peer pressure to be sexually active before they're ready. And most of that pressure comes from other boys.

You're thirteen and he's seventeen. Sure, you might feel really flattered that someone older wants to go out with you, but who has the power in the relationship? Often, it's not the younger person. And that's the problem with mismatched couples, no matter if it's age, experience, or anything else. If one person is making all the decisions, and there isn't a fair balance, say hello to a power struggle.

Not ready to get that close? It's okay. Chances are your friends are bragging about stuff that hasn't actually happened for them yet either. So just concentrate on what feels right to you.

Is it love or something else?

Love and respect. *Check.* Argue, but make up after. *Check.* Stamp out unhealthy stereotypes. *Check.* Now you know what a good relationship looks like. But what about an unhealthy one? Take a look at this "infatuation checklist."

- There's jealousy and mistrust.

- One person is put on a pedestal above the other.

- There's a lot of fear about losing the other person.

- You think that being part of a couple will make you more important.

- One person takes love but rarely gives it back.

Doesn't sound like love, does it? That's because it's not. Unhealthy relationships are built on a wobbly foundation of mean, controlling, disrespectful, hurtful, or even abusive behavior. He gets mad when you don't drop everything to be with him when he says he needs you. She criticizes your clothes, body, or personality. He keeps you from seeing your friends or from talking to other boys at school. Or maybe he forces you to do things sexually that you really don't feel comfortable doing, but you're afraid to say no because he threatens to dump you.

The weird thing about these relationships is that many of them seem to start out so well. He tells you you're gorgeous, and you believe him. She says you're the best thing that has ever happened to her, and you feel the same way.

But then, slowly, ever so slowly, it all breaks down. Maybe he says one day, "I like long hair on girls. Why do you cut yours?" And a small worm of worry starts to creep in. As the weeks or months go on, he seems less and less happy with your looks. It's subtle, though, and you get used to the jabs—although there's no way you would have been okay with them when you first started going out. But now? You feel bad about yourself and even wonder if what he says is true.

This type of relationship happens with a lot of regularity, by the way. According to one study, the majority of teens who have been in relationships—a whopping 61 percent—say that they've gone out with someone who made them feel bad or embarrassed about themselves.

"She's jealous because she cares so much about me, right?"
Wrong.
Jealousy is about controlling you, not loving you.

Don't go there

Here's a depressing statistic: one in three American teens say they've experienced physical, sexual, psychological (mental), or emotional violence in a romantic relationship. What's more, when the kids took the Centers for Disease Control and Prevention survey in the United States, 9.8 percent of them said their boyfriend or girlfriend had hit, slapped, or physically hurt them on purpose. Across the ocean, a 2010 British study suggested that a quarter of girls aged thirteen to seventeen had been physically hurt by their partner.

Violence is about control—who's more important in the relationship? Who has the power? Boys are sometimes taught that they do. They hear that "real men" don't let girls walk all over them or make them feel weak. Their buddies might even call them "whipped" just because they want to spend time with a girlfriend. After a while, these messages sink in and a boy might feel that he has to play the role.

Girls aren't always the victims, of course. While some girls use their fists to gain control, mind games are pretty powerful, too. Maybe she gets mad if her boyfriend or girlfriend talks to other girls, or she monitors text messages and phone calls. Maybe her partner "isn't allowed" to go to parties if she's not going.

No matter what form it takes, violence doesn't start all at once—it's usually a gradual thing. A boy tells his girlfriend that he doesn't like her new top. Soon he's saying she's fat or ugly. She feels worse and might start to believe it. The violence might even turn physical.

Because relationships are brand new right now, figuring out the rules can be tough. When is someone's obsession with you cute? When is it creepy? When does jealousy spiral out of control?

Here's the truth: hurting the person you're supposed to love is not cool. You know that. It doesn't make anyone stronger, tougher, or more in control. In fact, trying to control another person through violence or put-downs is usually a one-way ticket to the end of the relationship. And not only does it make everybody feel bad, it's also illegal.

NO VIOLENCE. EVER.

If anyone hits, punches, slaps, scratches, or hurts your body in any way, you need to get out of the relationship today and get help. Talk to an adult you trust. Or call a kids' help line. (There's a list of resources at the back of this book.) Getting support is important to your well-being, now and later on. Studies show that kids who were abused while dating are more likely to be physically hurt by a partner as an adult.

The time to stop the cycle is now.

Breaking up is hard to do

It's over. Maybe the boyfriend formerly known as Awesome Aiden decided he was into your best friend—and now they're going out. Or maybe you realized you just weren't ready for a girlfriend. You just want to hang out and practice hard with your swim team.

Even so, you find yourself crying in the bathroom at school when no one is there and hiding in your room when you get home. Whenever you hear the song you both really liked, you turn it off.

It's completely normal to feel this horrible. If your breakup seemed to come out of the clear blue sky, it's likely to feel even worse. We like to think we can predict how people will treat us, and feel especially hurt and angry when we find out we were wrong.

Stubbed toes and breakups

But is your emotional pain like the kind you feel when you, say, stub your big toe, or even break a leg?

Partly. Psychologists at Columbia University have found that intense emotional pain, such as grief or being rejected by someone you love, can actually flip the same switch in our brain that physical pain does. So when you broke up, your brain registered the message as a big ouch. To add insult to injury, a breakup also releases stress hormones that make us extra jumpy and upset.

Q: HOW DO YOU KNOW YOU'RE (FINALLY) GETTING OVER A BREAKUP?

A: You're no longer dreaming up new ways to get back with your ex. (It helps that the birds are singing, the sun is shining, and you laughed at a friend's bad joke for the first time in ages.)

When will this pain be over?

The emotional pain of a broken heart can last for a while. How long? Sadly, there's no strict mathematical formula that can give you that information. Let's say you only went out for three days, but it could take three months to kick your pining to the curb. Meanwhile, it might take only a few weeks to feel better after a relationship that lasted six months. You just can't predict these things—not only is everyone different, but every relationship is different as well.

Whatever your situation, you can take control and speed up the process so you can feel better again. Stick these tips into your bag of tricks.

TIP 1: Don't try to stop thinking about the person. Your brain needs a chance to get used to the idea that the relationship is over.

TIP 2: At the same time, don't spend too much time moping. Stick with your schedule, or better yet, do something you really love, like going to see a funny movie with your friends or heading out for a run. Laughter and exercise will both give you a happy boost.

TIP 3: Write in your diary (if you don't have one, start now). Take a good hour and spill out all your emotions on the page. Later, go back to your journal and write out all the things you learned from getting together and breaking up.

TIP 4: Share your thoughts with someone you trust—your best friend, your mom or your dad, your big brother—and don't be afraid to cry.

But if there's only one piece of advice you need to follow to get over a broken heart, it's this: **remember how awesome you are.**

Really. It's amazing how rejection can suck away confidence. Remind yourself of all the great things about you—your ability to play the flute by ear, the fact that you can run 3 miles (5 kilometers) without breaking a sweat, your talent for helping your friends feel better about themselves. If you're having a tough time remembering what your best traits are, just ask your friends. They'll tell you.

SOUNDS FISHY TO ME

There's an old saying people use after a breakup. Maybe you know it already?

"There are other fish in the sea."

This is supposed to make us feel better, because, hey, if we've been rejected by our honey, we can just find somebody new. There are plenty of fish—er, people—to choose from.

Well, this saying isn't so far off the mark. There are over seven billion people on earth today. And those fish? More than 360 marine scientists probed the oceans for a decade, did a little fancy math, and figured out that there are about 23,000 species of fish in our oceans. No word on exactly how many individual fish, from tiny microbes to sharks, that works out to be, but it's got to be a big haul.

The point is, there's going to be someone else out there for you, even if it doesn't feel that way right now.

THE BIG QUESTION

How do you know when your feelings turn into love?

It's about love, actually

**There's a lot more to sex than birds and bees.
Why does it have so much power?**

It seems simple enough. Take one penis and insert it into one vulva. Repeat. That's all sex is, right?

Well, if you're talking about sexual intercourse between a man and a woman, that's the basic idea. But sex is actually so much more than a simple math equation. Because one penis plus one vulva equals…what exactly? A baby? That's a possibility. But that's not where the story ends. Not by a long shot.

The reality is that sex—and human sexuality—is incredibly complex and has a huge impact on everything around you: the clothes you wear, how you think about love, and sometimes even the fights you have with your parents. (You want to date; they say that it's too early. Or you find out they want to buy your older sister condoms or put her on the birth control pill, and now you're completely freaked out!)

On a larger scale, take a look at the world's population. There are over seven billion people on this planet. Every single one of us is living today because two people got together and made decisions either on purpose or in the heat of the moment. That's a lot of sex...

And here's what else that number means: nearly everyone is a sexual person.

Q: WHY IS SEX SO EMBARRASSING OR EVEN SCARY?

A: Because we don't talk about it. When we don't talk about things, they can become shameful or scary. It's similar to the monster under the bed. As long as you are in the dark, that monster can seem terrible. If we shine the light on sexuality and talk about it, then we take the scariness away. It becomes just another part of our lives, another part of being human.

—*Julie Jeske, sex and relationship counselor in Portland, Oregon*

It's complicated

It's no surprise that sex is so popular. It can feel really good. So even if the end result isn't to add another person to the planet, there's a good chance you'll eventually do it because you'll enjoy the feeling it brings out in you.

That's because in a sexually healthy relationship, there are so many things at play. Intimacy. Happiness. Even a sense that you're respected and appreciated. Sex gives you lots of lessons about how to treat another with that same respect.

The truth is, sex can be a hugely powerful and wonderful force. That goes for everybody. Gay, straight, lesbian, bisexual. It doesn't matter.

So why does sex seem so complicated? That's because it can also be about...

Morality. Right and wrong. Good and bad. For example, some people feel that you're bad if you want sex, but you're good if you abstain.

Politics. Governments can tell us if one aspect of sexuality is illegal or accepted by society.

Crossed signals. Between the media, your parents, some religious beliefs, or even the sex education you get at school, you can get some very conflicting messages about what sex means. Throw them all together and it's no wonder you're confused.

Sex can also have a dark emotional side. It can make us feel...

Upset. Especially when sex is with the wrong person or happens at the wrong time. That also goes for when we feel pressured into going further than we feel comfortable with or doing something we don't agree with.

Worried and anxious. When your sexuality doesn't seem to match everyone else's around you.

Hurt. Sex can be used to put other people down so we feel better. Not cool.

Sick. Nobody goes looking for a sexually transmitted disease (STD)—such as herpes, HPV, or HIV—but they're out there. Condoms help keep us safer.

It's easy to feel overwhelmed when looking at all the ways sex can go awry. But here's another way of looking at it: if, despite all the negatives, people still want to get physical, what does that actually say about sex and sexuality?

You got it. It's an awesome thing.

Let's explore a few of those things that will make sex even better for you when it's something you're ready for and want to do. It's all about having the tools you need to make informed, personal decisions that make sense for you.

THE V WORD: GET IT RIGHT

A girl might call what she sees between her legs a vagina, but that's not entirely accurate. The vagina is actually the passage that leads from the opening of the vulva to the cervix. In other words, the inner part. The vulva is the sex organ—the part you can actually see. It's amazing how many girls and women (and boys and men) don't know the correct name for this part of the body. Kind of like calling your eyelid an eyeball. It's the right idea, but completely wrong.

Sexuality stages

No matter what you're doing or who you're doing it with, the feelings and changes in your body during sex usually follow this pattern:

DESIRE. You're interested in getting it on with someone you're attracted to (or even solo).

EXCITEMENT. You're getting aroused because parts of your body, not to mention your brain, are being stimulated by touching, nibbling, kissing, sucking, and grasping. You know, the fun stuff.

ORGASM! It doesn't get much better than this. An orgasm happens when your arousal (sexual excitement) is at its peak. Suddenly you're not thinking, just doing. Your mind goes blank and you feel like a million bucks as you ride this amazing sensation for as long as it lasts. Usually a boy or man will ejaculate when he has an orgasm, but not always. And usually a girl or woman will have to have pressure put on a part of her body called the clitoris (a small bump near her vulva that's filled with nerve endings) to have an orgasm.

One more thing: just because you start at desire, it doesn't mean you have to get all the way to the orgasm stage. Sometimes you're not ready to go there. Or maybe you've already tried it but feel more comfortable sticking with kissing and touching.

Either way, it's important to listen to your gut and do what you feel like doing—not what your girlfriend or boyfriend wants you to do. Even if you've already had sex with a person in the past, it does not mean you've got to do it again right now if you don't want to. And it's okay to stop at any time if things just don't feel right at all.

ORGASM SMORGASM

As if. Let's be frank here, once somebody has an orgasm the first time, it's pretty rare to feel "meh" about the experience. So let's break down the whole electric, tingly thing.

What is an orgasm anyway?

Well, let's start with what it's not: ejaculation. (Girls have orgasms, too, right?) Although usually boys will ejaculate when they have an orgasm (or "come," as a lot of people call it), sometimes they don't. In basic terms, an orgasm is the climax of sexual excitement.

What does it feel like?

Back a few decades ago, a scientist did a study on orgasms and found that women described them as beginning with a sense of waiting or suspension (kind of like, "whatever this is, it's gonna be good!"), quickly followed by intense pleasure that begins at the clitoris and spreads out in the pelvis. The area feels warm and tingly and then that feeling starts to move through the body. Some say they feel muscles contract in their vulva, vagina, and lower pelvis.

Boys feel a lot of the same things. It starts with warm, deep pressure, and it leads to a point of no return when they can't stop themselves from ejaculating. Again, there's a feeling of intense pleasure and a pumping sensation. With boys, there's also a warm rushing sensation when semen travels through the urethra inside the penis.

So are orgasms different for boys and girls?

Well, yes and no. That same study discovered that although men and women are made differently (duh!), they actually experience orgasm in roughly the same way. They know this because they wrote down orgasm descriptions from men and women but took out references to the actual body parts. Then they asked experts (therapists, doctors, and others) a question: "Can you tell which one is written by a male and which one is written by a female?" Guess what? They couldn't do it with any accuracy. In other words, the experts often got it wrong.

There are differences, though. Women, on average, tend to take longer to get to the orgasm stage than men. And while boys and men usually have only one orgasm and then enter a recovery phase, far more women have been known to have more orgasms a short time later. Just remember, despite what a lot of movies show, most women don't end up having an orgasm through sexual intercourse alone. Remember the clitoris? It's full of nerve endings and is where orgasms happen for most women.

Masturbation (touching your own genitals) is a funny thing. Not only does it feel good to explore your penis or clitoris and vulva, but it can be a healthy way to learn about your body, pleasure, and what you like. But some people feel really uncomfortable even saying the word.

Still, what you might find out about yourself through masturbation is important because everybody's desires are so different. It might be a good idea to know what turns you on before having a romantic and sexual relationship.

- You're a girl, and as you read a sexy eBook, you notice a pumping sensation between your legs. Hello. That feels good! Knowing what you were thinking about at the time might come in handy someday when you need to tell your partner what you like.

- Or maybe you're a guy and as you're masturbating you realize your hands aren't enough to send you over the edge. Instead, you've got to visualize that cute girl or boy who makes you feel electric. That emotion and your passions? They're connected. That's good to know, too.

You don't have to masturbate, obviously. That decision is completely up to you. But if you do, just know you're definitely not the only one. A 2011 study from Indiana University shows the following:

- 63 percent of younger boys said they masturbate
- 43 percent of younger girls said they did, too
- 80 percent of seventeen-year-old boys said they masturbate
- 58 percent of seventeen-year-old girls copped to it, too

So masturbation is a major way kids, teens, and adults express their sexual side. (Even though not everybody will admit they do it.)

Not just about sex

Yeah, let's start right there. Sex can be a lot of things, which is why the whole topic can be confusing.

- Maybe your friend hooked up with someone at a party and went all the way. That's sex.

- Or maybe someone you know has had oral sex (when mouth and genitals meet). Some people think of that as sex, too.

- For others, though, when they say "sex" they mean that someone else has contact with another person's sex organs or genitals. The vulva, the penis, the vagina, the anus. Any of them, or all of them.

- And how about masturbation? That's when you touch your own body and genitals to feel good. Is it sex if you make it all the way to an orgasm? What do you think?

Really, when it comes to sex, the only thing that's the same for everyone is that it's different for everyone.

Speaking of emotions and feelings, how does love have an impact on sex? That all depends. Let's be honest here. It's not always true that you're going to feel that soul-defining feeling with every person you get close to in a sexual way. Although that will definitely be the case many times and hopefully for the person you end up with.

The main thing to remember is to love yourself no matter who you're with. That means being true to yourself and respecting your own values. Because if you do that, and have a sense of humor if the experience isn't exactly the way you expected it to be, you'll still come away from that sexual encounter feeling good.

That's how Val Barr, a sex educator in Calgary, Alberta, in Canada, sees it. Whenever she's talking to people about making any kind of decision around sex, she says it's important to check in with three parts of you:

HEAD—ask yourself this:
Why am I doing this? Do I agree with what is going on here? Does it fit with my values and boundaries? How will I feel about this decision tomorrow?

HEART—ask yourself this:
Does this feel right to me? Do I like this person and feel comfortable and safe around him or her? Can I trust this person?

BODY—ask yourself this:
What does my body want to do? Do I like what's happening and am I—and my partner—protected from pregnancy and sexually transmitted diseases (STDs)?

"In the end you have to ask yourself if what you're doing is lined up with your head and your heart. If it is, it's a healthy decision," she says. "If it's not, you'll get this niggling feeling. That's a good clue you actually want to delay and think first."

For instance, how do you feel about oral sex? Maybe your friends are all for it. Or maybe your friends are saying, "No way would I want that! And I don't want to give it either."

Forget everybody else. How do you feel? Knowing what you think, feel, and believe about something like oral sex before it happens can make things a lot easier on you if you're in that situation. You'll be less likely to cross your own line if you already know what that line is.

Sure, the line can get moved around a bit, but you're the only one who should be able to shift it.

Consent is... about reading body language and being certain that your partner is as into what you're doing as you are. Yes doesn't just mean yes—it's an enthusiastic yes!

Consent is not... about trying to convince someone to do something they seem uncomfortable with. Sex is never about being a challenge that has to be overcome.

One more thing: if you knew your boyfriend or girlfriend didn't like to be sexual that way, would you still push it? What does that mean about how you see the person? As you've read in other chapters, respect, love, and, yes, sex connect.

And while we're on the subject of respect...

Beware the relationship-busting monster!

That would be another way to describe a gender stereotype—the one thing that rips apart otherwise lovely romantic relationships. You'll find them popping up all over the place when people fall in love, especially in first relationships.

Here's the Godzilla of them all:

She's a slut. He's a stud. Hmm. This one is so popular, and it has been for ages. Girls aren't supposed to like to explore their sexuality. But boys? They're only after one thing. (And it ain't your mamma's brownies.)

So is it true? Of course not. Some girls do like sex. Some boys want to wait. Then why is this idea so ingrained in the way many boys and girls and men and women see each other? Part of it is that most kids and teens don't have other relationships to compare to. All they have are messages they get through TV. Music videos. Poorly informed friends. Porn.

There it is. The P word. And there's a very good chance your older brother, sister, cousins, or friends have seen it. Maybe you've even seen it, too.

IT'S CALLED SEXUAL ASSAULT

If anybody—even somebody you know well—ever touches you without your permission or gives you unwanted sexual attention (showing you pornography, asking you to expose yourself, talking a lot about your body), tell someone. Yes, it can be tough. Chances are, you'll feel confused, numb, ashamed, or even blame yourself afterward. Don't. Sexual assault can happen to anyone—girl, boy, straight, gay, bi, transgender, young, and old. No one is allowed to touch you without your permission. Ever. That's why there are laws to protect you.

TIP: Want to talk to someone who can help? You can usually find the number of your local sexual assault help line by searching for "YOUR CITY/TOWN + sexual assault help line."

Pornography—pictures and movies that show people having sex or doing sexual things—is known for keeping gender stereotypes alive and well. If you find (or look for) pornographic images on your computer, you might think those images portray how sex works. Even how people treat each other.

The thing is, pornography is all about fantasy. It's not real.

You know who is? That girl or boy you're locking lips with. That person has feelings and desires that might surprise you. The fun and exciting part is finding out what they are.

AND NOW A WORD FROM BLAKE SPENCE, WISEGUYZ SEXUAL HEALTH PROGRAM COORDINATOR…

"If you have access to pornography, you're not going to get in trouble for that. There's a time and a place for pornography in some people's lives. But if you use it as sex education and expect what you've seen to be like real sex in real life, that's a problem. What you see in pornography is not real or even appropriate in so many ways. It's not how women are treated. It's not what sex looks like."

Learning more from all the right places

Sexting, stereotypes, and exploring what you value—these are heavy topics. So who exactly is supposed to be teaching you about all this stuff? Some people believe it's the parents' job. Others feel schools should be involved. What do you think?

If you have questions (and everybody does), you need answers. Many teachers today do a great job explaining how your body works and how to protect yourself from STDs. That's a good start. At the same time, many schools in North America are committed to teaching kids that they should stay virgins until they're married, no matter what. This is called abstinence.

There's nothing wrong with wanting to stay a virgin for as long as it makes sense to you. There are a lot of good things about waiting until you're 100 percent ready for sex. It prevents pregnancy and STDs, for one. Abstinence is also a good way to postpone taking any risks with your health, your emotions, and even your reputation—at least until you're better able to handle them. Saying no to sex with your boyfriend or girlfriend means you've probably had a conversation about how far both of you are ready to go. Kissing? Touching? More? And you can keep having that healthy conversation as time goes on and you feel more comfortable together.

Sending racy images of yourself out to your boyfriend might sound like fun, but is sexting a good idea? How about posting the photo on your Facebook page for your friends? No way! Here's why: all it takes is one friend of a friend to send that image out to someone else and you've lost control of it forever. It could go out to people you don't even know on the other side of the planet, or, even more terrifying, to kids in your school or your parents.

But maybe abstinence shouldn't be the last word on the subject. Many people find that it's difficult to wait for a long time when their bodies seem ready to have sex. (And if you've decided you will be a virgin and you cave suddenly, you may be less likely to have protection, like a condom, with you.)

Ultimately, the decision to have sex or to wait is up to you and you alone.

If you want more information about sexuality and how it has an impact on your life, don't be afraid to ask someone you trust. Or keep doing what you're doing now: read and search for more information that helps you make sense of what's happening to you during puberty.

Your body is the best gift anybody could ever give you—or that you could give another person. Love it. Explore it. Take care of it.

Do that, and everything else takes care of itself.

THE BIG QUESTION

If you knew for a fact that your best friend had an STD and he or she started going out with someone new, would you tell that person?

→ Conclusion

The end is just the beginning

Maybe you don't know this, or maybe you do, but puberty is a hot topic in the news today. Weird, huh? Something as old as life itself is still making headlines.

While I was researching this book, every single day magazine and newspaper articles, Web sites, videos, podcasts, books, and college papers crossed my desk. Some of them were trying to sort out weird puberty conundrums, like why girls and boys seem to be hitting puberty earlier than ever. Others asked some big questions, such as, "Who should teach sex education to kids: parents or teachers?" or "When do kids know that they're transgender?"

Even after reading all the way to the end here, you probably still have questions of your own. A lot of these are probably difficult to bring up with just anybody because they're embarrassing or very personal. Or you just want to seem like you know all the answers already.

That's why you'll find this list of Web sites you can visit for more information helpful.

LEARN MORE

Body Changes

kidshealth.org/kid/grow
Wondering why your body is growing and changing? This Web site, offered by Nemours, an American children's health organization, will answer a lot of your questions.

pbskids.org/itsmylife/body/puberty
What's puberty and what does it do to your body, brain, and emotions? Well, this book covers all of that and more, but if you still have questions, check out this site from PBS Kids. Bored? Do the puberty crossword puzzle. Seriously. This site has one.

Self-Esteem and Body Image

mediasmarts.ca/body-image/body-image-introduction
Learn more about girls, boys, and body image here.

about-face.org
Don't fall for the media circus! About-Face gives women and girls tools to understand and resist harmful media messages that affect their self-esteem and body image.

Self-Esteem and Body Image

youth.gov.au/bodyImage/Documents/ ConversationStarters_StudentLeaders.pdf
Want to be a leader and create a body-image–friendly school? Sure, this link is kind of long, but this document offered by the Australian government gives you everything you need to get a conversation started with your friends and help everybody feel better about themselves.

Stress, Emotions, and Depression

mindcheck.ca/mood-stress
Are you stressed? Take the quiz and find out. Lots of useful information about stress, anxiety, and depression.

kidshelpphone.ca/Teens/InfoBooth/ Emotional-Health/Depression.aspx
If you're feeling stressed and depressed, this site is a good place to find out how you can start to feel better. If you live in Canada, you can call the toll-free line and talk to a real person who can give you some help, too.

au.reachout.com/Helping-a-friend-with-depression
Maybe you're not the one going through depression, but your friend is. Here's a site that can give you tips for helping someone else. It offers information to help you take care of *your* feelings and moods, too.

Eating Disorders

eatright.org/kids
Learn how to eat a healthy diet and feel good, too. Scientifically based health and nutrition information is a few clicks away.

ChooseMyPlate.gov
Track your food with this site and see how your diet measures up.

nedic.ca
The National Eating Disorder Information Centre in Canada is the place to go for information, statistics, and a checklist to see if you or a friend has an eating disorder.

Bullying

stopbullying.gov
The US government's comprehensive site for kids, parents, and teachers. Understand what bullying is and how to stop it—there's even a number to call if you live in the United States and need to talk.

netsmartzkids.org
Give cyber-bullies the boot with this site and learn how to use the internet safely.

bullying.org
Use this site to learn a ton about why kids treat other kids badly and what to do about it.

canadiansafeschools.com/students/ overview.htm
If you're being bullied, you're not alone. The Canadian Safe School Network can help!

Being Gay

pflag.org
American organization for parents, families, and friends of lesbians and gays. It has support hotlines, too.

pflagcanada.ca
Canadian? Here's the super-helpful and supportive site for you.

youcanplayproject.org
You Can Play Project. Gay athletes. Straight allies. Teaming up for respect.

Healthy Relationships

blog.loveisrespect.org
Your friend is dating someone who is controlling, jealous, and suspicious. What should you do? Visit this site for loads of information about how to build healthy relationships and put an end to dating violence and disrespect. Check out the "Power and Control" wheel.

plannedparenthood.org/health-topics/ birth-control-4211.htm
Planned Parenthood is a great resource if you have questions about birth control, relationships, and even body image.

whitehouse.gov/1is2many
Just say no to dating violence.

TALK IT OUT!

Got problems? Feeling upset and want to talk to someone right now? Many countries around the world offer real-time help for real-life problems that kids experience every day.

For instance, in the United States there's the Boys Town National Hotline (and, yes, girls can use it, too) at 1-800-448-3000. Counselors take calls about depression, suicide, bullying, divorcing parents, and even gang violence. In the UK, kids call ChildLine at 0800 1111. In Canada, if you're younger than twenty, you can call Kids Help Phone at 1-800-668-6868, a toll-free, 24-hour counseling and referral service. The calls are anonymous, so you can say whatever's on your mind.

Too shy to talk? Many of these services also let you email questions or even chat over IM and get to-the-minute advice from counselors.

People I want to thank...

Like puberty itself, a book on the topic doesn't happen overnight, or without loads of support. That's why I'm over-the-moon grateful to all the amazingly insightful people who offered their time, expertise, and ideas. Tori, Nicole, Laura, Analee, Erin, Alta, and Emmy—thanks for giving me a window into your world and sharing a few slices of pizza with me. This book is for you (literally). A big thank-you needs to go out to the good people at the Calgary Sexual Health Centre, Val and Blake, for their insight and support. You know your stuff. Many thanks go to all the other experts and researchers who gave time to be interviewed for this book: Patricia Adler, Fiona Dunbar, Dr. Lisa Hicks, Rob Frenette, Julie Jeske, Dr. Margaret Lumley, Dr. Moss Norman, Lynn Peril, Vandana Sheth, and Steven Solomon. A special thank you goes to Barbara Leavitt. Thanks to Dr. Hoover Adger for his professional insight. Dave and Dayle, you get big-time kudos for keeping life running smoothly even when I had to step out of the day-to-day for a while. Ann Douglas, Teresa Pitman, and especially Amy Baskin, thanks for keeping me on track and letting me talk about stuff you'd rather forget! In fact, I'd like to give a pat on the back to the dozens and dozens of people who opened up to me about their puberty experiences as I was writing this book.

And, John, how in the world could we have known that this book would take so many twists and turns? Without your thoughtful guidance, this one would still be circling around my twisted brain.

Finally, this one goes out to all the kids on the planet who go through puberty (read: all of you). Especially my own two children, Nathan and Nadia, who now beg me to stop writing books until I've at least taken them on a Disney cruise. You drive a hard bargain!

Growing Up, Inside and Out grew up because of people like you.

~ *Kira*

Editorial consultant

Jennifer Munoz, BSW, RSW
Health Promotion Facilitator, Alberta Health Services

Bibliography and sources

We used a wide variety of helpful resources and material to develop this book. Some ended up being especially useful—and helped us understand bodies and feelings in a whole new way.

Abraham, Laurie. "What If Our Kids Really Believed We Wanted Them to Have Great Sex?" *New York Times Magazine*, November 20, 2011.

Alder, Patricia, and Alder, Peter. "Dynamics of Inclusion and Exclusion in Preadolescent Cliques." *Social Psychology Quarterly* 58:3 (1995): 145–62.

"Ben Cohen's Anti-Bullying Push in US." *BBC News*, May 27, 2011. www.bbc.co.uk/news/world-us-canada-13567781.

Bielski, Zosia. "In the Age of Internet Porn, Teaching Boys to Be Good Men." *The Globe and Mail*, April 21, 2012.

Concordia University. "Boys and Their Bodies [Press Release]." September 26, 2011.

Callender, Mary P. "Marjorie May's Twelfth Birthday, 1929." Museum of Menstruation & Women's Health.

Carpenter, Siri. "Sleep Deprivation May Be Undermining Teen Health." *American Psychological Association Monitor*, October 2001.

Chen, Cynthia, et al. "A Community-Based Study of Acne-Related Health Preferences in Adolescents." *Archives of Dermatology*, 2008.

Cloud, John. "Why Girls Have BFFs and Boys Hang Out in Packs." *Time*, July 17, 2009.

"Coming Out." Calgary Sexual Health Centre. Online.

Davison, K. K., and Birch, L. L. "Weight Status, Parent Reaction, and Self-Concept in Five-Year-Old Girls." *Pediatrics*, 2001.

DeHaan, Laura. "Bullies." North Dakota State University, March 2009.

Derenne, Jennifer, and Beresin, Eugene. "Body Image, Media, and Eating Disorders." *Academic Psychiatry*, 2006.

Dobbs, David. "Beautiful Brains." *National Geographic Magazine*, October 2011.

Douglas, Ann. "Should Sex Educators Teach Good Sex?" *The Toronto Star*, April 23, 2012.

Eastwick, Paul. "Sex Differences in Mate Preferences Revisited: Do People Know What They Initially Desire in a Romantic Partner?" *Journal of Personality and Social Psychology* 94 (2008): 245–64.

"Eating Disorders 'Rife in Girls.'" *BBC News*, September 4, 2001. http://news.bbc.co.uk/2/hi/health/1523129.stm.

Elliot, Andrew. "Red, Rank, and Romance in Women Viewing Men," *Journal of Experimental Psychology: General* 139:3 (2010): 399–417.

Fagot, Beverly, and Hagan, Richard. "Aggression in Toddlers: Responses to the Assertive Acts of Boys and Girls." *Sex Roles: A Journal of Research* 12:3–4 (1985): 341–51.

Fattah, Hassan. "Why Arab Men Hold Hands." *The New York Times*, May 1, 2005.

Fox, Kate. "The Flirting Report." *Social Issues Research Centre*, 2004.

Fuxjager, Matthew. "How and Why the Winner Effect Forms: Influences of Contest Environment and Species Differences." *Behavioral Ecology*, 2010.

Glass, Ira. "449. Middle School." *This American Life* audio, October 28, 2011.

Glenn Lilley, Terry. "Healthy Relationships: Teen Dating Violence Curriculum." 2003. Online.

Government of Alberta. "Homophobic Bullying." Online.

Government of South Australia. "Breasts: Kids' Health Topic." January 2011.

Greenberger, Dennis, and Padesky, Christine. "Mind Over Mood." *The Guilford Press*, 1995.

Grohol, J. "Another Way Women Choose a Romantic Partner." *Psych Central*, 2008.

Grossman, Lev. "The Secret Love Lives of Teenage Boys." *Time*, August 26, 2006.

Healy, Melissa. "Bucking Gender Expectations: For Kids, It's Relatively Common." *Los Angeles Times*, February 23, 2012.

Hoffman, Jan. "Boys Will Be Boys? Not in These Families." *The New York Times*, June 10, 2011.

Horstman, Judith. *The Scientific American Book of Love, Sex and the Brain: The Neuroscience of How, When, Why and Who We Love.* Jossey-Bass, 2011.

Izzo, John. "Every Day Should Be Pink Shirt Day." *Vancouver Sun*, February 29, 2012.

Jayson, Sharon. "Truth About Sex: 60% of Young Men, Teen Boys Lie About It." *USA Today*, January 26, 2010.

Juntti S.A., et al. "The Androgen Receptor Governs Execution, but Not Programming, of Male Sexual and Territorial Behaviors." *Neuron*, April 2010.

Keyes, Allison. "What If Your Child Says, 'I'm in the Wrong Body'?" *Tell Me More* audio, December 26, 2011.

Kirchner, Mary Beth. "Tom Girls." *This American Life* audio, February 13, 2009.

Lock, James, and Le Grange, Daniel. *Help Your Teenager Beat an Eating Disorder.* The Guilford Press, 2005.

Lohr, Steve. "Photoshopped or Not? A Tool to Tell." *The New York Times*, November 28, 2011.

Luscombe, Belinda. "The Science of Romance: Why We Flirt." *Time*, January 17, 2008.

Madaras, Lynda, and Madaras, Area. *My Body, Myself for Girls.* Newmarket Press, 1993.

Marcus, Mary Brophy. "Cosmetic Surgeries: What Children Will Do to Look 'Normal.'" *USA Today*, June 25, 2009.

McLeod, Saul. "Conformity." Simply Psychology, 2007. http://www.simplypsychology.org/conformity.html.

Mead, Nicole, et al. "Social Exclusion Causes People to Spend and Consume Strategically in the Service of Affiliation." *Journal of Consumer Research* 37:5 (2010): 902–19.

Melnick, Meredith. "Girl, You Are So Not Fat! Does 'Fat Talk' Make Anyone Feel Better?" *Time*, March 31, 2011.

Meston, Cindy, and Frohlich, Penny. "Love at First Fright: Partner Salience Moderates Roller-Coaster-Induced Excitation Transfer." *Archives of Sexual Behavior* 32:6 (2003): 537–44.

Paul, Annie Murphy. "Life After High School." *Time*, June 20, 2011.

Neill, Fiona. "Boys' Voices Are Breaking Earlier; Girls Are Developing Breasts as Young as Six. But Why?" *Intelligent Life Magazine*, Summer 2010.

Nemours Foundation, The. "How Cliques Make Kids Feel Left Out." Online.

Nicholson, Jeremy. "Just Asking for It! Part 1." *Psychology Today*, May 13, 2011.

Nicholson, Jeremy. "You Don't Say: Persuasive Body Language for Flirting and Dating." *Psychology Today*, May 6, 2011.

Orenstein, Peggy. "Playing at Sexy." *New York Times Magazine*, June 11, 2010.

Orloff, Judith. "The Health Benefits of Tears." *Emotional Freedom: Liberate Yourself From Negative Emotions and Transform Your Life.* Three Rivers Press, 2011.

Park, Alice. "Found! The Seat of Embarrassment in Your Brain." *Time*, April 18, 2011.

Park, Alice. "Why the Pain of Romantic Rejection Feels Like a Punch in the Gut." *Time*, March 28, 2011.

Pearce, Tralee. "Mean Boys." *The Globe and Mail*, September 30, 2008.

Pendergrast, Mark. *Mirror Mirror: A History of the Human Love Affair with Reflection.* Basic Books, 2003.

Peril, Lynn. "Growing Up and Liking It: A Primer of Period Pedagogy, 1868–1996." Museum of Menstruation & Women's Health, 1997.

Perry, Susan, and Vernacchio, Al. "Hook-Ups and Hang-Ups." *Independent School*, 2010.

Pryor, Liz. *What Did I Do Wrong? When Women Don't Tell Each Other the Friendship is Over*. Simon & Schuster, 2006.

Reaney, Patricia. "Neanderthals Sped through Puberty." *Reuters*, April 29, 2004.

Reppenhagen, Michael. "Study Finds Health Benefits from Strong Mom-Son Relationships." *The State Press*, September 6, 2010.

Rushowy, Kristin, and Kennedy, Brendan. "Kids Not Safe from Bullying, Expert Says." *The Toronto Star*, September 27, 2011.

Safe Start Center. "Teen Dating Violence." http://www.safestartcenter.org/resources/teen-dating-violence-month.php.

Sax, Leonard. *Boys Adrift: The Five Factors Driving the Growing Epidemic of Unmotivated Boys and Underachieving Young Men*. Basic Books, 2009.

Shaffer, Susan Morris, and Gordon, Linda Perlman. *Why Boys Don't Talk— and Why It Matters: A Parent's Survival Guide to Connecting With Your Teen*. McGraw-Hill, 2005.

Something Fishy Website on Eating Disorders, The. "Eating Disorder or Diet?" http://www.something-fishy.org/whatarethey/edordiet.php.

Spilsbury, Louise. *Me, Myself and I: All About Sex and Puberty*. Barron's Educational Series, Inc., 2010.

Stromberg, Peter. "Why Do We Get Crushes on Both People and Stuff?" *Psychology Today*, September 6, 2009.

Szalavitz, Maia. "Mind Reading: Using Peer Pressure to Change the World." *Time*, April, 8, 2011.

"The Ethics of American Youth: 2010." Josephson Institute: Center for Youth Ethics. http://charactercounts.org/programs/reportcard/2010/installment01_report-card_bullying-youth-violence.html.

Tugend, Alina. "Peeking at the Negative Side of High School Popularity." *The New York Times*, June 18, 2010.

Villarica, Hans. "How Retail Therapy Works: Spending Money for Social Acceptance." *Time*, October 12, 2010.

Villarica, Hans. "The Tricky Politics of Tween Bullying." *Time*, December, 3, 2010.

Wallis, Claudia. "Does Puberty Make You Stupid? Lessons from Mice." *Time*, March 22, 2010.

Wallis, Claudia, and Dell, Kristina. "What Makes Teens Tick?" *Time*, September 26, 2008.

Way, Niobe. *Deep Secrets: Boys, Friendships and the Crisis of Connection*. Harvard University Press, 2011.

Wedekind, Claus, and Dustin Penn. "MHC Genes, Body Odours, and Odour Preferences." *Nephrol Dial Transplant* 15:9 (2000): 1269-71.

Weir, Kirsten. "Fickle Friends: How to Deal with Frenemies." *Scientific American*, June 16, 2011.

Wong, Jan. "Why Aren't Schools Teaching Kids about the Pleasures and Perils of Sex?" *Toronto Life*, February 3, 2012.

World Health Organization. "Male Circumcision: Global Trends and Determinants of Prevalence, Safety and Acceptability." Department of Reproductive Health and Research and Joint United Nations Programme on HIV/AIDS (UNAIDS), 2007.

→ Index